IN THE FOOTSTEPS OF BODHISATTVAS

IN THE FOOTSTEPS
OF BODHISATTVAS

BUDDHIST TEACHINGS ON THE
ESSENCE OF MEDITATION

Phakchok Rinpoche

SHAMBHALA

Shambhala Publications, Inc.
4720 Walnut Street
Boulder, Colorado 80301
www.shambhala.com

Cover art: Courtesy of Robert Beer
Cover design: Daniel Urban-Brown
Interior design: Gopa & Ted2, Inc.

9 8 7 6 5 4 3 2 1

First Edition
Printed in the United States of America

⊗This edition is printed on acid-free paper that meets
the American National Standards Institute z39.48 Standard.
♻This book is printed on 30% postconsumer recycled paper.
For more information please visit www.shambhala.com.
Shambhala Publications is distributed worldwide
by Penguin Random House, Inc., and its subsidiaries.

Library of Congress Cataloging-in-Publication Data

Names: Rinpoche, Phakchok, 1981– author.
Title: In the footsteps of Bodhisattvas: Buddhist teachings on the
essence of meditation / Phakchok Rinpoche.
Description: First edition. | Boulder, Colorado: Shambhala, 2020.
Identifiers: LCCN 2020004887 | ISBN 9781611808377 (trade paperback)
Subjects: LCSH: Tripiṭaka. Sūtrapiṭaka.
    Samādhirājasūtra—Commentaries. | Bodhisattvas. | Samadhi. |
Meditation—Buddhism.
Classification: LCC BQ2087.R56 2020 | DDC 294.3/85—dc23
LC record available at https://lccn.loc.gov/2020004887

The earth can break open with its mountains and forests

and the ocean waters can likewise part;

the sun and moon can fall to the ground,

but the speech of the Victorious One never changes.

—THE *KING OF MEDITATION SUTRA*, CHAPTER 14

CONTENTS

FOREWORD

THE FACT that Shakyamuni Buddha was born in this world and taught the dharma is a great fortune for those who connect with his teachings. We can still read and hear the Buddha's words and, with the guidance of living lineage masters, apply his instructions directly to our minds. For Buddhist practitioners, the primary and essential root of our practice is the texts that preserve the words of Shakyamuni Buddha, as well as the commentaries that elucidate the meaning of those precious words. There are tremendous blessings available to us when we make his teachings the basis of our personal dharma practice.

Phakchok Rinpoche has taken the Buddha's words from the *King of Meditation Sutra* as the basis for his teachings in *In the Footsteps of Bodhisattvas*. Since the Buddha's own words are the purest source of the dharma, we can be sure that these teachings will take us on a path that leads to the lasting happiness of awakening. I am very happy that Phakchok Rinpoche has written this book, and I request you to study these words, take the instructions found herein to heart, and apply them sincerely and directly to your personal experience. If you do this, they will undoubtedly bring great benefit.

Chokyi Nyima Rinpoche
Boudhanath, Kathmandu, Nepal
May 22, 2020

EDITOR'S PREFACE

WHOEVER APPLIES the instructions contained in this book can move from fear and discontentment into confidence and joy. It contains the very heart of Buddhist meditation practice, distilled by an authentic Buddhist master and offered to anyone who harbors the wish to become a lamp for this confused world. These teachings were given by Phakchok Rinpoche across the globe over the course of several years. I recall an intimate group of students sitting on the floor of Rinpoche's living room in Boudhanath, Nepal, drinking tea under a wood-worked shrine filled with precious statues handed down from Rinpoche's ancestors, listening raptly as he elaborated on the essence of compassion. At Rinpoche's retreat center in Cooperstown, New York, in the height of summer, Rinpoche used the root text of the *King of Meditation Sutra* to vividly show his students the true meaning of meditation. In a cozy apartment, beside an autumnal Central Park, Rinpoche described how things appear to a mind that is free from suffering. In each of these instances Rinpoche took us to the core of the Buddha's wisdom by relying on the words of the historical Buddha, Shakyamuni.

The teachings attributed to the Buddha are called *sutras*, and this book is based on the sutra called the *King of Meditation* (also known by its Sanskrit title, *Samadhiraja Sutra*). This sutra is considered to be one of the most influential of all the Buddha's teachings on meditation in the Mahayana school of Buddhism. Mahayana Buddhism, or the "Great Vehicle," teaches that enlightenment dawns when we realize the indivisibility of emptiness (*shunyata*) and great compassion (*mahakaruna*). Emptiness here refers to the fact that we are unable to find anything stable or permanent, either within ourselves or within so-called outer phenomena. Great compassion refers to compassion that has no reference point—something akin to an unconditional love. The Buddha says that we can realize this profound unity when we develop the correct conduct, meditation, and discerning wisdom. The *King of Meditation Sutra* contains powerful teachings on precisely these three topics; it can therefore reliably guide us into the sustained and indestructible meditative realization that is free from suffering.

Samadhi is often roughly translated as "meditation" and *raja* as "king," which is why the *Samadhiraja Sutra* is commonly called the "King of Meditation Sutra." While it is convenient to equate the word *samadhi* with "meditation," Phakchok Rinpoche doesn't want us to reduce our understanding of samadhi to a state of absorption or feel-good voidness. Throughout the course of this book, Rinpoche reminds us again and again that the highest samadhi is beyond absorption and beyond concept. It is naturally present when you bring together the correct view of reality, authentic meditation practices of the Buddha, and supremely altruistic activity. It is enhanced through the cultivation of loving-kindness, compassion, joy, and equanimity. It is unearthed through skillfully discerning who we are, what we are made of, and where we are going. In this book we learn how to engage in such practices and investigations, so that we can naturally let go into the unity of emptiness and compassion.

This book is organized around Phakchok Rinpoche's favorite quotes from the *King of Meditation Sutra*. Rinpoche sifted through his personal copy of the sutra and selected lines from the Tibetan that he felt were most potent for his own training. He then asked Oriane Lavole of Lhasey Lotsawa Translations and Publications to render these lines in English. These quotations are not presented in the same order as they appear in the root text, which is many hundreds of pages long. Instead the compilation has been distilled and organized as a path of training for Phakchok Rinpoche's students and readers. These are the words of the Buddha. They are to be contemplated, savored, and applied within our own experience.

This is a book for beginner practitioners as well as for those who have made the Buddha's teachings the core of their lives. It is perfectly suitable to read this book from front to back while sequentially spending a week, two weeks, a month, or a year on the exercises at the end of each chapter. It may also be helpful to open to any of the chapters and glean inspiration from the words therein.

Overall, this is a book that is brimming with wisdom—

not the tired and dusty wisdom of an old library, but the dynamic and responsive wisdom that is undeniably present in the eyes and actions of Buddhist adepts. This book is imbued with the lucidity of Phakchok Rinpoche and his long lineage of enlightened teachers, stretching all the way back to the Buddha himself. These are the oral instructions from teachers who have walked the path from suffering to bliss and have imparted their wisdom to Phakchok Rinpoche. He now gives this wisdom to us.

Whenever Rinpoche gave these teachings on the *King of Meditation Sutra*, he seemed to overflow with courage. That is the gift of the Buddha's words. These teachings give us the courage to skillfully tread the gnarled path of our lives to arrive at the blissful home of awakening. This is the path of the bodhisattvas, and here we are, invited to walk in their footsteps.

It was with great compassion that Kyabgon Phakchok Rinpoche asked me to help compile these instructions. Any errors or faults in this text are totally mine. Any benefit that comes to you from reading this book is fully Rinpoche's kindness.

Jack deTar
New York City
October 8, 2019

Acknowledgments

I WOULD LIKE to express my appreciation for Kyabje Khenpo Rinpoche. When I first started reading and studying the *King of Meditation Sutra*, he answered many of my questions and revealed why this text is one of the pillars of the Tibetan meditation tradition. He comes from an older generation of meditation masters and has a deep respect for this sutra. The fact that he has such appreciation for the *King of Meditation Sutra* should inspire his friends and students to study these words. I would also like to thank Jack deTar for his help in writing this book. I would like to thank my secretary, Joshua Fouse, for his consistent help in all things, and Oriane Lavole for her translation of the root text quotations and her efforts on behalf of Lhasey Lotsawa Translations and Publications. Alan Pope and Libby Hogg worked hard to edit this manuscript; I am thankful for their efforts and I also appreciate the work of the many sangha members who transcribed my teachings throughout this whole process.

In the Footsteps of Bodhisattvas

INTRODUCTION

THIS IS NOT a book about a one-dimensional type of meditation training. Instead, this book teaches how the intangible essence of meditation naturally arises when we properly line up the right conditions within our lives. This essence is compassionate and blissful but totally ungraspable; yet it can be realized. Don't you want this?

To gain this realization of reality that brings total freedom, we need to practice the primary teachings of the Mahayana Buddhist path. We cannot focus on a singular meditation technique and expect to have a fruitful result if we extract it from the framework of correct view, meditation, and conduct. Instead, we must align all of the dimensions of our lives with authentic practice. This is what in Buddhism is called "walking the path." If we are able to do this, there is no doubt that we will realize the open heart of true meditation.

As in other Dharma books, we will find here exercises and meditation methods; but we will also find the words of the Buddha, sourced from the *King of Meditation Sutra*, organized into a clear path of training. The sutra itself is forty chapters long, from which I have selected my favorite quotes and compiled them in this text. If we spend time reflecting on these passages and we apply the instruction and methods offered in each chapter, we will undoubtedly experience positive results. After all, we are studying and practicing the words of the Buddha.

Unless we are Buddhist scholars with a library of sutras, how many of our Dharma books actually give us the Buddha's words? We read many quotations from great masters, but how often do we work with quotes directly from the Buddha in our daily lives? Through reading and savoring the Buddha's words, we gain a special confidence and dignity from knowing what he specifically taught. When I personally rely on the teachings of the Buddha, insight into reality comes.

THE MAHAYANA PATH

This sutra does not belong to a particular lineage; it belongs to everyone. You can be generally interested in meditation, a student of Soto Zen, Tibetan Buddhism, or any other school of Buddhism and this teaching can help your practice. The *King of Meditation Sutra* is, however, a Mahayana scripture, or a scripture of the Mahayana tradition, or Great Vehicle of the Buddha's teachings. The Mahayana path is called "great" because it takes as its goal the liberation of every being from suffering and because it leads to the realization of the twofold emptiness of the self and of phenomena.

At the core of the Mahayana path is *bodhichitta*, or the awakening mind of compassion. Bodhichitta is divided in terms of the two truths of reality—that is, the relative and the ultimate. Relative bodhichitta is what we train in while on the path, and it further comprises two parts: the bodhichitta of aspiration and the bodhichitta of application. The bodhichitta of aspiration refers to cultivating the mental states of loving-kindness, compassion, joy, and equanimity, which are boundless. Through training in these attitudes our mind becomes altruistic and stable. The bodhichitta of application refers to practicing the six perfections: generosity, discipline, patience, joyful effort, and meditation, all of which are embraced by the sixth, wisdom. Through training in these we benefit others and arrange positive conditions in our lives that support our practice. This book teaches us how to unify all of these practices in order to give rise to ultimate bodhichitta, which is none other than the completely enlightened state, the supreme samadhi.

THE *KING OF MEDITATION SUTRA*

I first studied the methods of meditation when I was ten years old, but effective practice didn't begin for me until I was sixteen, and still it was another three years before I began to experience real benefit, such as becoming more mindful and compassionate. At twenty-one, I came across the *King of Meditation Sutra* as part of my studies at Dzongsar Shedra monastic university in India. However, it wasn't until I was thirty-one that I actually began an intensive exploration of the text, which has continued for the past seven years. When I began to investigate the text in detail, I saw that so much of what I had been studying, reflecting upon, and practicing throughout my life was directly related to this sutra. I also discovered that in this Mahayana sutra the Buddha teaches methods we use in the Vajrayana, the tradition of Tibetan Buddhism. I hope that when Vajrayana practitioners recognize aspects of their own methods in this book, it will increase their confidence in their own practice.

Some of us think of ourselves as practitioners of the meditation tradition known as Mahamudra. If you think of yourself like this, please know that the Mahamudra path is actually the result of the teachings of the *King of Meditation Sutra.* The sutra itself is not organized like a traditional Mahamudra manual; such manuals came hundreds of years after this sutra was written and were developed by great masters on its basis. The Mahamudra manuals traditionally give sixty sequential stages of practice. This sutra is not like this. Instead it includes questions and answers between the Buddha and bodhisattvas—those traveling the path of complete awakening through cultivating bodhichitta. The *King of Meditation Sutra* includes instructions on how to skillfully behave, how to skillfully think, and how to use the seemingly material world as a support for your training as well as clear advice on how to get out of the way so your innate wisdom can come naturally.

The sutra itself is full of stories that cut directly to the essence of meditation, what it refers to as samadhi. For thousands of years it has been the companion volume of monks, nuns, yogis, and household practitioners. I want you to learn meditation from this source, to connect to the Buddha and begin to train just like the meditation masters of the past.

THE MESSAGE OF MAHAYANA SUTRAS

Just like the famous *King of Meditation Sutra*, the Buddha taught many sutras at Vulture Peak. Actually, many of the Buddha's seemingly disparate teachings complement each other in a mind-blowing way. For example, we can understand the intent of this *King of Meditation Sutra* by looking at how it relates to the popular *Heart Sutra*.

The *Heart Sutra* describes the state of buddhahood. When you hold the *Heart Sutra* in your hands you are actually holding the Buddha's state. When you read the *Heart Sutra* you see statements like ". . . no path, no wisdom, no attainment, no nonattainment . . ." and so on. Reading this, you might think, "What kind of craziness is this? Clearly the Buddha taught a path and methods, and gave all sorts of teachings through which we can be free from our suffering, so what's going on here?" This is what the *Heart Sutra* is saying: Everything is mind, mind is empty, the empty nature is clarity, and clarity is awareness. Pure awareness is buddhahood; the state of buddhhood doesn't have a path; that state doesn't have attainment; that state doesn't have nonattainment. That state is free from the five aggregates of form, feeling, perception, formation, and consciousness, which constitute our entire experience.

If we have been lucky enough to receive instructions on how to encounter this liberated state of pure awareness through meditation, we are not able to maintain it for very long, only perhaps a few seconds. So, the *Heart Sutra* describes the enlightened state, but it doesn't teach us how to practically get to it.

I often teach another sutra entitled the *Wisdom of the Time of Death Sutra*. This sutra is very short and offers condensed instructions on achieving the state described in the *Heart Sutra.* There was an ancient Tibetan king who used to read the *Heart Sutra* every day in order to clarify his view of reality, but he also used to read the *Wisdom of the Time of Death Sutra* to guide his meditation practice.

Now, here is a key point: Just as the *Heart Sutra* is the condensed form of the 80,000 stanzas of the *Perfection of Wisdom Sutra*, we can say that the *Wisdom of the Time of Death Sutra* is the condensed form of the *King of Meditation Sutra.* So we can look at this quote from the *Wisdom of the Time of Death Sutra* to understand how we will learn to meditate in this book based on the *King of Meditation Sutra*:

> Akashagarbha, at the time of death, the bodhisattva should train in the wisdom of the time of death. The wisdom of the time of death consists of the following: Since all phenomena are naturally pure, cultivate well the notion of lack of existence. Since all dharmas are contained within bodhichitta, cultivate well the notion of great compassion. Since all phenomena are naturally luminous, cultivate well a

mind free of reference point. Since all entities are impermanent, cultivate well a state of mind that is not attached to anything at all. When the mind is realized, that itself is wisdom. Therefore, cultivate well the notion that Buddha is not to be searched for elsewhere.*

This instruction is very profound. It summarizes all of the points of training of the Mahayana path. Through the teachings on the *King of Meditation Sutra*, we will learn to apply each of these statements fully and directly.

THE ESSENCE OF MEDITATION

The twenty-first-century world should understand that true meditation gives rise to complete freedom. If we don't understand this, then we are in danger of diluting the idea of meditation down to a simple session on the cushion to make us feel calm. If we are in pursuit of freedom from suffering and wishing for a profound relationship to reality, then all experiences of our lives must become meditation. I want readers to take the view and meditation practices outlined in this book as a path, or as a strong support for the authentic meditation tradition they are currently

* Prajnasamudra and Santideva, *The Noble Wisdom of the Time of Death Sutra*, trans. Lhasey Lotsawa Translations and Publications (Nepal: Lhasey Lotsawa, 2015), 5–7. https://lhaseylotsawa.org/books/the-noble-wisdom-of -the-time-of-death-s%C5%ABtra-and-commentaries.

practicing. These methods have worked for countless practitioners who came before us and they will work for us too.

Everything you see and hear and experience can be meditation, unceasingly. I want this text to give you the real instruction. I hope it will benefit you directly and immediately. Personally, the *King of Meditation Sutra* affected me very deeply.

I want this book to make beings truly happy. I hope the merit of this book will be a cause for the pure aspirations of the buddhas and bodhisattvas—those who have completed the path and experience the highest meditation, the king of samadhis, to come true.

1
THE KING OF SAMADHI

It is the wisdom path of the buddhas;

the seal of all phenomena;

perfect, omniscient wisdom.

—CHAPTER 1

THE BUDDHA once stayed with a large assembly of bodhisattvas on the holy mountain of Vulture Peak in Northern India. It was there, among the piled boulders and under the open sky, that he is said to have taught many of the Mahayana sutras. Countless beings gathered to sit before him and receive his wisdom.

One day, as the Buddha rested in the realization of ultimate reality, a particularly handsome bodhisattva, Youthful Moon, walked over to the Buddha. He respectfully knelt and requested the Awakened One to turn the Wheel of Dharma by giving a teaching on the perfect way to practice meditation. He wanted to know the most perfect conduct, the most perfect meditation, and the most perfect wisdom.

The Buddha, brimming with delight, gazed at the bodhisattva and said that because he, the Buddha, is awakened, he is able to teach Youthful Moon. The Buddha told Youthful Moon that there is a samadhi, a meditation, that brings complete realization, total understanding, and the natural development of countless qualities: the samadhi of great equality. To the joy of everyone there the Buddha then began to teach the *King of Meditation Sutra*, which perfectly explains how we go from ignorance to enlightenment.

Going beyond Samsara

The sutra teaches us to be naturally virtuous, gentle, and loving. It teaches us how to see clearly, to speak clearly, how to consider the Buddha's teachings, and how to sustain the power of mindfulness. It leads to the exhaustion of habits and shows us how to go beyond the pain of samsara, the endless cycle of suffering. First, we train in the methods of the *King of Meditation Sutra* in order to realize the ultimate meditation. Then our life naturally becomes this meditation.

We want to gain wisdom. We want our minds to be like mountains, unshakable. We do not want to go backward in our Buddhist practice. Instead, we want to be virtuous and reduce our negative behavior. We want to know the minds of others so that we can help them. We wish to renounce the world of pain. We do not want weak and lonely minds. We want to know how to understand the Dharma and how to tame the mind. We want to know how to resolve conflict in our lives and in the lives of others. We want to see the natural purity of everything. If we can do this, we will be joyous. Actually, we will be beyond joy and conventional happiness.

This ultimate samadhi or meditation taught by the Buddha on Vulture Peak is not a state of being absorbed. It is not cultivated, not a type of mental film that we superimpose over everything in our lives. It is unfabricated—the recognition of the true nature of reality. It is the vividness of our mind's empty nature that lacks any permanent identity, that is simply pure awareness.

CREATING POSITIVE CONDITIONS

In order to attain this realization, we create positive conditions that support its unfolding, which is described in the sutra in the passages below.

> Not to hold those who suffer in contempt, but to give them wealth; not to despise the impoverished; to have compassion for those of poor discipline; to benefit beings by means of helpful gifts, loving-kindness, and the Dharma; to give material things.
>
> —CHAPTER 1

This training is not just about long hours on the meditation cushion; it is a path walked with every moment of our being. We walk this path by exercising skill on the relative level—we become better people, without hypocrisy. In a sense, we become genuine and real, while at the same time we turn toward the ultimate.

> Being skillful; letting go of characteristics; discarding concepts.
>
> —CHAPTER 1

To be skillful requires mindfulness. Here, "mindfulness" means discerning what should be adopted and what should be abandoned. We need to become aware of our negative and positive mental states. We must plainly know whether we are harming or benefiting others and ourselves. In order to do this, we observe our motivations. We become skilled in abandoning harmful states of mind and good at creating the merit of positive mental states. This kind of mindfulness requires continuous cultivation and joyful effort, the fruits of which are the supportive conditions for the dawning of insight within our formal, seated meditation sessions.

THE PATH OF REALIZATION

When it comes to meditation, the Buddha told Youthful Moon that the practice begins with focusing on the representation of the Buddha's body. The Buddha instructed us to settle the mind on the form of the Buddha (in our case this will be a visualization of the Buddha) and become open to the sublime qualities represented by that form. In this way, we develop the power of concentration that is then applied to investigating the mind. After we have investigated the mind, we develop the strength of our realization of emptiness by letting go of specific characteristics of phenomena as unchanging and fixed.

> Relying on emptiness; relying on the lack of characteristics; realizing the essence of wishlessness.
> —CHAPTER 1

When the strength of our realization has developed, we discard concepts altogether. After we have discarded concepts, we rest in the reality in which nothing remains to be said.

> Blessed by the Buddha,
> you will know ultimate reality.
> Knowing ultimate reality,
> there is nothing left to say.
> —CHAPTER 11

Through discarding concepts we obtain fearlessness, we expand the clear awareness that is free from concepts, and we maintain pure discipline.

> Obtaining fearlessness; spreading the light of wisdom and having pure discipline.
> —CHAPTER 1

There is no higher realization than this. By connecting with the sutra that teaches this method, we connect with the actual Buddha, which is the awakened mind.

We may sometimes fear the path, not understanding what it means to renounce or abandon our habits. There are many who experience this fear. It helps to remember the Buddha's words: If it is worldly bliss and happiness that one seeks, then practicing what is taught in this *King of Meditation Sutra* will surely bring worldly bliss. If it is the bliss of an arhat that one seeks, one will attain the bliss of going beyond the afflictions of negative emotions. If one's goal is to become a fully awakened buddha, then practicing this profound samadhi will lead to total mental purification, vast wisdom, and the unspeakable power of full awakening.

> It destroys all perceptions,
> and is therefore called samadhi.
> It does not give rise to afflictive emotions;
> it is pure, clear, and luminous,
> unshakable and unconditioned:
> the domain of bodhisattvas.
>
> —CHAPTER 13

2
ONLY THE "I" IS PAINFUL

Whoever has ego-clinging
is in a state of suffering.

—CHAPTER 14

IN OUR CARS on the way to work, at restaurants, or in conversation with our family members, we so often feel attacked. We fear injury, we fear suffering, and we fear hell. The truth is we dip into hell all the time. We dip into hell whenever we freak out and are worried, which is almost always the case. The expectation of aggression from others drains our energy and puts us into a state of panic.

We end up in hell because we are attached to countless conditions that are definitely going to change—conditions that have no substantiality in the first place. These conditions, such as the color of our hair, the youthfulness of our skin, or the quality of our clothes, are the basis for our belief in a real "self." We may search the entire world, trying on many costumes and meeting many people, and still we will not find the self. We search for a true "me" at the center of our experience, but no matter what senses we rely upon to find it, the "me" is nowhere to be found. We can try to taste the self with our tongue, or smell the self with our nose, or see it with our eyes, but still we can't point to it and say, "That's it!" Don't just believe what I'm saying—look! Can you locate the true, unchanging self?

1ST: LOOK FOR THE SELF IN THE BODY

Eyes, ears, and nose are invalid.
Tongue, body, and mind are invalid.
If these faculties were valid,
what would be the good of the noble path?

—CHAPTER 9

This body is the main reason we believe in a solid and real "me." Consider this: there is not a single thing that is not composed of other things. Every object is made of parts, and each part is made of more parts, and this continues indefinitely. We see a form and call it a chair, but when we search for the object "chair," where is it? We can say there is a flat wooden seat with a wooden back and four legs, all held together with nails. We can isolate a leg and look for its essential "leg-ness," but we will only find a composition of wood fibers. And if we go deeper, we will find atoms and subatomic particles, and further infinite potential division. If we subject our body to the same analysis, we find it is likewise nothing more than an aggregation, a composition of many parts.

So, there are some questions to ask. Is your body you? If so, what part of the body? How about your hand: Is that you? What is your hand made of? Skin and bone and blood and nerves? If you chop it off, have you chopped off a part of your self? At what point in chopping up the body will you be cleaving the actual self? But if you say that the self is not in the body, then where does the self reside?

Now, in the Mahayana, although the body is a strong condition for attachment to the mistaken belief in a self, it is not considered fundamentally bad. The problem is attachment to the body, which creates complications and distractions. Most of the time, when we commit unvirtuous actions, they are in the service of the body. Theft and violence, for example, often come from a desire to safeguard our bodies. Though it is not the totality of our experience, the truth is that we will inevitably experience sickness, old age, and death. Accidents involving our bodies or the bodies of our loved ones are unavoidable. The Buddha said that we can learn to see how meaningless it is to remain overly attached to this physical body by remembering that it is destined to decay. On top of this, we should realize that we cannot find a single, whole, truly existing entity to call "my body."

2ND: LOOK FOR THE SELF IN THE MIND

One might try to identify the mind as the self. But any attempt to find the "mind" is also fruitless. It is free from the five senses. If we try to say that the mind is this way or that, that it has a color or a shape or a smell, that it is inside or outside the body, we end up failing. Even so, this mind that is so difficult to see creates all the facets of our present life. All our suffering is created by something that we can't even identify. Because self does not exist, all our efforts to reify and protect it with the hope of gaining lasting happiness are doomed from the beginning. We need to realize selflessness in order to be altogether free from attachment. Only then will we stabilize the samadhi of great ease.

> Seeing the suffering of beings
> who claim a multitude of views,
> you teach the Dharma of selflessness
> in which there is no good or bad.
> —CHAPTER 14

The Buddha divided suffering into physical suffering, mental unhappiness, and destitution. For example, imagine you wake up one morning and roll out of bed, and even before your feet touch the ground you experience searing pain, as if someone just rammed a knife in your belly. That is the first category: physical suffering. You realize you have to go to the doctor to find out what is wrong with you. After hours of analysis and blood tests, the doctor says you have an incurable, horrible disease. The pain that comes with this information is mental suffering, or what is sometimes called "suffering upon suffering." On top of all of this, you don't have any insurance or money for treatment, and you become totally depressed. This is the pain of destitution.

All of this suffering comes from believing that there is a truly existent person who has truly existent stomach pain, who has a truly existent disease, who is truly helpless. Of course, we must acknowledge that we do need positive material conditions to support our practice at this point and that material conditions do contribute to our relative sense of well-being. This example is simply meant to show how through the realization of selflessness there would be nobody to be afflicted. How convinced are we of this?

The best way to become convinced of this type of suffering is by looking at the relationship between mind and the sense of self in day-to-day life. Look at how your belief in a self determines almost every word coming from your mouth, every move you make, every thought you think. To look in this way is to practice mindfulness. My teacher used to say that if you don't have mindfulness in your daily life then you are a pile of dung. He actually said that. He said that without mindfulness you are simply a pile of dung and you smell very bad, but you don't know it. Without mindfulness, you suffer and you spread suffering.

Until you are convinced that the mind is the most valuable thing of all, the Dharma will not be so important to you. But one day it might just click. When that happens, I am going to be right beside you, without you seeing me, knocking on the door of your head, and I will be saying, "Welcome to Dharma!"

The mind that is not in meditation is conceited;
meditation itself is the second type of conceit.
Without conceit, you gradually engage in awakening;
mindfulness without conceit is supreme Buddhahood.

—CHAPTER 13

In the *King of Meditation Sutra*, the Buddha tells Youthful Moon that to meditate on the nature of selflessness is to rest in a state in which conceit is entirely absent. When we are not engaged in meditation, we are in a conceited state of mind. Yet when we sit down and compose the body to meditate on some *thing*, a subtle conceit also remains. What to do? We need to find whatever it is that is not a state of conceit, for that is the genuine mindfulness of the Buddha. The state in which conceit is absent is enlightenment. In this state of the absence of conceit, even the *idea* of "selflessness" is not present. Note that this state is not a vacuum or a dark nothingness. Rather, it is the awakened state.

In order to approach this awakened state, we need to reach an understanding of how the buddhas and bodhisattvas are inseparable from us. In Tibetan Buddhist practice, we first visualize the buddhas and bodhisattvas, and then we visualize that they dissolve into us. Many people ask, "How can the Buddha dissolve into me? I am a bad person; I do many terrible things." I always tell them the same thing, which is "Yes, maybe we do have a lot of negativity inside us. In the midst of all that badness, though, there is a core of goodness, and that goodness is the intrinsic nature, which is unconditioned and does not constitute a singular self."

"Do you love your husband?"

"Yes."

"Do you love your child?"

"Yes."

"Do you have compassion for your neighbor's barking dog?"

"No."

So there's the point. You love your child, you love your husband, and you hate your neighbor's dog when it is hungry. This means you have some innate good qualities, but that your qualities are limited by the conditions related to your concept of what suits "me." How to develop those innate good qualities? Gain trust in the potency of your present qualities and understand where they come from. In Buddhism we have this saying: "If someone wants to search for water, they have to listen for the sound of the water falling; if they want to locate the fire, they have to follow the smell of the burning wood."

3RD: UNDERSTAND THAT COMPASSION IS SELFLESSNESS

Whether we are religious or not, we all have some kind of feeling that compassion is right. If we see something that hurts another person, it seems to hurt us too. Of course, we can also be brainwashed into thinking that killing is good—in the name of ideals, country, religion, and so forth. But generally, we know what is harmful and what is helpful. Compassion steadily grows from this intuitive sense of selflessness—perhaps at the core we are not solid and separate selves, perhaps we really do share the same nature.

I heard a story that I think you may have come across already. During the First World War there were many soldiers who intentionally missed their shots, because they didn't want to kill their enemies. The commander would say, "Fire! Fire!" and some of the soldiers would shoot and secretly try to miss their targets. I even heard that during one holiday, although both enemy armies were entrenched, they came out and smoked cigarettes together and drank coffee and talked. They even played a game of football in the no man's land between their trenches. But when the holiday was over, they returned to their sides and continued fighting.

Even at the heart of war, most of us don't want to slaughter each other. Often military language shows this. Instead of saying, "We killed the enemy," soldiers are taught to say, "The target was neutralized." There isn't such a big problem with the word "neutralized," but "kill" makes us feel something. I don't mind neutralizing, but I do mind killing. During the American Civil War, there were several cases in which one soldier shot another soldier, and as the smoke cleared, he went down and offered medicine and bandages to the man he had just shot! That is human nature. Another example comes in the case of a good friend of mine who is an excellent kickboxer. He is very strong and agile and has broken the noses of many people, but the idea of hunting small animals makes him wince. He doesn't like it. He feels genuine compassion for them. Deep inside our hearts we have a feeling that violence and cruelty are wrong. This comes from an intuitive sense that we are not independent selves. That is exactly in accordance with the Buddha's teaching.

This feeling is a sign that our whole nature is enlightened. It is a feeling that can arise without any spiritual training because it is actually the way things are. Most cultures and religions emphasize a respect for life. It's the basic, foundational thing. Of course, sometimes one crazy guy will say crazy things and activate negative patterns within people, and they will fall under the spell of his words. But for the most part, ethics look similar all over the world.

My teacher said that if you look at our planet, there is only one type of animal that will follow the lead of another of his species into complete stupidity, and that animal is the human being. I responded by saying human beings are the smartest creatures. He smiled and told me that in one sense they are very intelligent and in another sense they are idiots. One stupid person can rise up and everyone will follow him—but show me an animal that can be completely brainwashed by the speech of another animal.

When you just sit where you are, even if you are not contemplating Dharma or considering spiritual things, you can have quite a sincere mind. You can enter into a very fundamental disposition in which you understand that doing right is right and doing wrong is wrong. You can consider the Buddha's teaching to be the development of that intrinsic knowing, that moral compass. If you have compassion for your family, if you feel they are somehow not distant, not so separate from you, if you hurt when they hurt, then you can try to expand this feeling to the rest of society. Try to expand this feeling to all the strangers you pass on the street, to all the birds outside, even to all the pundits arguing on the television.

If you do something good for your children and try to be free from expecting some reward, that is Dharma. When many parents do something good for their children, they have expectations. "I did this for you! I worked so hard! And now this is how you repay me?" It is often like this. Some don't verbalize it, but most feel it. It is normal. Dharma, however, is this: Do something good, and that in itself is good. Don't ask for any reward. Don't build up the self that feels a need to be repaid. Don't expect returns. This is the part of the Buddha's teaching that leads to the development of pure compassion. The Buddha explains selflessness so that human beings can become better, healthier, and free.

The most important part of this teaching is to realize that you have the capability to improve because you are not a fixed entity. If you apply focus to your compassion practice, your compassion will grow. If you put effort into your meditation practice, insight into selflessness will develop. With effort and attention, insight has no choice but to develop. When compassion and insight develop, samadhi dawns.

Knowing one, you know all;

seeing one, you see all.

However much you may teach,

no arrogance will ever come from this.

—CHAPTER 11

If you know the absence of your own self, you begin to know the absence of all selves. It becomes easier to move out, to expand. In this expanding taste of compassionate emptiness, you contact the great samadhi.

Understanding Selflessness

Search for the identity of "I" from as many angles as you can.

1. Look within the body.

2. Look within the mind.

3. Look within the space surrounding you.

4. When you don't find "I," be aware of this, and let go.

3

RENOUNCING SUFFERING

1ST: RENOUNCE LIKE A WOUNDED DEER

By discarding riches as one would spit out saliva,
and desiring solitude and remaining in the wilderness,
those who give up afflictions and overcome obstacles
will realize stainless, unconditioned awakening.
Buddhas and bodhisattvas as numerous as grains of
   sand in the Ganga—
whoever pays them homage for millions of eons,
and one day renounces household life with great
   weariness—
that person is supreme.

—CHAPTER 5

I F YOUR CLOTHES caught fire and you felt the flames singeing your hair and burning your skin, you would quickly search for water to put out the fire. The Buddha tells us to give up worldly life with this same speed. With renunciation in our hearts, we go to a place of solitude like a wounded deer bedding down to heal. The pain of our impermanent

lives is great, and our need to realize stainless, unconditioned awakening is also great.

In solitude we have fewer distractions and greater space
to cultivate positivity. The Buddha clearly explains the benefits of going into isolation. There is less activity of the
body. There are fewer distractions of the mind. There are
none of the tensions that arise from debating others. There
are less harmful forces. There are fewer factors that can stir
up negative emotions. One becomes calmer. Discipline is
naturally present. In solitude, you truly wish to practice the
Dharma. In solitude, you liberate yourself.

> I have opened wide the door to bliss:
> I have explained the nature of phenomena as it is
> and taught exactly how rebirth comes about
> as well as the benefits of nirvana.
> If you consistently discard unvirtuous friends
> and rely on a spiritual master;
> avoid crowds and remain in forest dwellings;
> continuously cultivate a loving mind;
> always keep pure discipline;
> take joy in training and always exert yourself;
> and practice generosity and wisdom,
> you will have no difficulty in obtaining this samadhi.
> —CHAPTER 4

In the Foundational Vehicle of the early Buddhist traditions, the Buddha mostly refers to the practices of monks
who renounce worldly life and physically isolate them-

selves from it. There isn't much mention of householders gaining spiritual accomplishment. It is true that from a practical point of view, the life of a monk is beneficial for training. A monk has less outer work and fewer responsibilities. He therefore naturally has less attachment and a better chance of realizing the truth. If you have many things to do, you cannot focus one-pointedly on the Dharma. It is a fact that wherever you direct your attention is where you gain success.

2ND: RENOUNCE LIKE A DREAMING KING

Whereas the Foundational Vehicle emphasizes physical renunciation of worldly life, in the Great Vehicle, renunciation has to do with acknowledging that samsara is like a dream: This type of renunciation is entwined with the understanding of the ultimate truth of emptiness. When you gain the experiential understanding that ultimately you never die and are never born, and that you would never find the actual essences of things even if you were to search for them for centuries, then there is nothing worldly to be attached to whatsoever. Through study, reflection, and meditation, you will eventually come to experience this directly.

We are enmeshed in the karmic effects of our activities because we do not realize the ultimate view. Consequently, each of us experiences the results of our positive and negative actions. When we renounce according to the

Mahayana, we renounce clinging to ourselves and to substantiality altogether in order to gain the liberation that allows us to benefit others.

> Giving up even my own self, I will accomplish the benefit of beings.
>
> —CHAPTER 30

Personally, I am a householder, married with a wife and children. Yet the Buddha told us to abandon everything, to literally fear home. When we hear these teachings, we sometimes think, "I will try my best." If we strictly follow the scriptures, we can have the sense that despite being attracted to the Buddha's teachings, we aren't really practicing correctly because we aren't monastics. We can have the feeling that we can't possibly advance our spiritual path given our lifestyle. A tension arises by the idea of renouncing our family, which makes us feel distressed and frustrated. This seems to be wrong, and yet so much of the Buddha's teaching seems right. Given that the core of the Buddhist teachings is nonattachment, we may wonder how we can reconcile practicing as a layperson when we bear such tremendous responsibility for our loved ones. The important thing to understand here is that nonattachment has nothing to do with withholding love from our families or abandoning our responsibility to them.

On the level of the *vinaya*, which are the Buddha's teachings pertaining to the conduct of monks, the physical and verbal objects and expressions of attachment are what must be cut. Renunciation within this context refers to the idea that if you like something, you should get away from it. Therefore, in the vinaya you will not find a monk-king or a monk-businessman. In the Mahayana teachings, however, practice focuses more on inner conduct, or motivation. Nonattachment may still be reflected in outer dress and behavior, but we often see examples of lay people who are awakened beings, such as bodhisattva kings, who broaden our understanding of nonattachment beyond leaving behind worldly possessions. Though monks are forbidden in the vinaya from touching gold, Nagarjuna himself is said to have changed iron into gold in order to support his monasteries. There are many stories like this. They show that on the bodhisattva level, nonattachment has to do with the mind.

During the time of the Buddha, King Indrabhuti confessed that he could not give up worldly life. Indrabhuti had a massive kingdom and many subjects, all of whom depended upon him and his skill as a ruler. The Buddha told the king that it was indeed possible to be a ruler and still develop renunciation and taught him the essential meaning of renunciation. Indrabhuti took this essential meaning and integrated it into his life without abandoning his responsibilities to the people who depended upon him.

Generally, renunciation is associated with "abandoning," but in this context it can also mean "being free." We "abandon" everything, but we need not literally dispense with all our material possessions. If we tossed away our house and clothes and coffee machine, it's possible we would create positive conditions for practice—but this is not a practical option for most people. Instead, what we must take to heart is that when we hear the word *renunciation*, we should think *freedom.*

The Tibetan emperor King Trisong Detsen had three sons, and each ruled the kingdom while receiving teachings from Padmasambhava, who is credited with bringing many of the Buddhist teachings originally to Tibet. Despite being surrounded by princely wealth and power, they were practicing nonattachment because their minds were set on awakening, on "freedom." They worked toward awakening, not for themselves, but for all beings. So as long as you keep in your heart the thought "I want to achieve awakening for the sake of all beings," you will always be practicing the essential meaning of renunciation.

As you progress in your understanding, nonattachment can become complicated, because the thought "I really want to get out of samsara" is ultimately an obscuration. If you really want to get away from something, it shows that you have aversion to some *thing.* It shows that you still believe in substantiality. It shows that you don't see that there is nothing in reality to get away from. The moment you recognize there is ultimately nothing to abandon is when you find genuine freedom and nonattachment. Through training in samadhi, you will give rise to this recognition.

3RD: CHECK YOUR RENUNCIATION THROUGH THE EIGHT WORLDLY CONCERNS

Untarnished by the eight worldly concerns,
their body is pure and their actions immaculate.

They have few desires, firm contentment,
and no attachment. They possess the buddhas' qualities.

—CHAPTER 17

This passage refers to the qualities of *bodhisattva mahasattvas*, great practitioners who have advanced on the path of awakening. Success in the practice of samadhi is intimately connected with our conduct. Proper conduct improves our ability to gain meditative insight. Conduct means the way we deal with the eight worldly concerns. The eight worldly concerns are the desire for fame, praise, happiness, and material gain, and conversely, the wish to avoid insignificance, criticism, suffering, and loss. If you take a look at the eight worldly concerns, you will see that on a fundamental level they all come down to aversion, attachment, and ignorance. Anything worldly has to do with these three feelings.

The great masters of the past have said that the eight worldly concerns are what show us our progress along the path of abandoning desire. The normal world does not consider desire to necessarily be a negative thing, but the spiritual world, the world of meditators, acknowledges that desire always eventually brings pain.

We can check the progress of our practice on several levels. These are the view level, the motivation level, the meditation level, the conduct level, and the fruition level. When great practitioners of samadhi evaluate their renunciation, their question is: "How much ego-clinging is present in my daily life?" If ego-clinging is as strong as the last time they checked, then they can tell that their practice has not improved, or some aspect of the practice has not been addressed. On the level of motivation, these practitioners look inward to see what is driving their practice. At the level of meditation, practitioners of samadhi check how much distraction and dullness is present during a session and evaluate their ability to apply the antidotes to overcoming these difficulties. On the level of conduct, they check the strength of their mindfulness that guards against the eight worldly concerns. When it comes to the level of fruition or result, they check whether they have great hope to achieve realization or fear of losing realization. If hope or fear are present, then they clearly have not achieved fruition. Now, if they are able to proceed toward the result but remain unattached within that aspiration, then that is the genuine approach to fruition. This is the question we should ask ourselves: "Am I maintaining the state that is free from attachment to the result?"

I will be honest—if you really have the strong resolve to be unattached to the eight worldly concerns, then you are a good practitioner. Conversely, if you have neither the wish nor intention to throw off the eight worldly concerns, but you still want to practice samadhi, you are a poor practitioner. The ancient Tibetan Kadampa masters were superior practitioners with incredibly powerful mind training (*lojong*). They worked their minds until they became completely flexible, until they could toss out the desire for gain as though it were spit. The foundation for their training originated in India, stemming from the Mahayana scriptures, such as the instructions in this *King of Meditation Sutra*.

Truthfully, you cannot practice the path without detaching from the desire for fame and respect. You cannot practice the path correctly if you hanker after praise and gain. Your samadhi will simply not improve if you remain attached to these wishes.

This topic does not apply only to Dharma practitioners. Everyone struggles with the eight worldly concerns—this is why they are called "worldly." Most people want respect, praise, or money in order to improve their lives. When they have money, they want increased fame and reputation. If we don't keenly observe the ferocity of these underlying motivations as we begin to engage in spiritual practice, then spirituality itself becomes the tool by which we feed aversion and attachment.

Aversion and attachment are not so difficult to see. Somebody says, "Oh, you are very handsome." Right away, you like it. Of course, you can try not to like it, but you do like it. Likewise, if someone says you are ugly, immediately you feel upset. If you are a practitioner, your training might prevent the arising of full-blown anger, but you may still experience difficulty managing your emotions for a short time. Such moments can be windows into how our practice is going. The next time someone insults you, compliments you, or ignores you, look directly at your reaction and observe your emotions.

Seeking no gain and fearing no loss;
desiring no pleasure, opposing no displeasure;
enjoying no praise, disliking no blame;
coveting no happiness and avoiding no suffering.

—CHAPTER 1

Our attachment to the eight worldly concerns becomes more subtle and sneaky as we advance along the path. For me, since I am now a teacher many people prostrate to me, so it appears I am somehow special. On top of this, people often praise me and tell me I am a great person. As we progress along the path, people will recognize the qualities that come from the Dharma and equate those qualities with you as a person. This becomes a strong cause for attachment among advanced practitioners. However, if you look at many ancient Buddhist treatises, you can see right away that their authors are often self-deprecating. These masters say, "I am not a great writer. I wrote this just to benefit myself, but if anybody else benefits I will be quite happy." They never praise their own qualities or even hint at the eloquence of the text they have composed. This shows that they are maintaining the essence of the practice.

Tibetan masters remain so mindful of the threat of the eight worldly concerns that sometimes when two realized lamas enter a shrine room together, they will argue with each other, each trying to persuade the other to take the higher meditation seat.

Whoever does not have excessive attachment
to this hollow life and limb
has vanquished the host of *maras*
and will reach awakening at the foot of the Bodhi tree.
The body is empty and selfless,
and life is a dream, tremulous as a drop of morning dew.

—CHAPTER 22

I was recently in a movie theater, and everyone around me was crying. A woman a few rows away was sniffling, and the man beside her had tears in his eyes. I observed everyone—for two hours they were completely stuck in the film. They were totally attached to what was happening two-dimensionally in front of them. When we watch a movie, we drink in the emotions of the characters. Though we see a screen and acknowledge that the people in the story are actors, we still cry! Our emotional response is quite independent from our reasoning.

Ultimately, emotions are a display of ignorance. You might ask, "Really? Every emotion?" To which I would reply, "In a sense, yes." Whether an emotion is positive or negative, it is a blind movement of the mind—it is a reaction. I have many emotions. I know that these emotions are happening, but I keep having them because the continuum of thought is never-ending. If we don't work with our minds, then our habits are refreshed all of the time, and their grooves deepen. If you reduce your thinking, it will be difficult for habits to solidify. What is nourishing your lust, for example? Would you experience the actual sensation of lust if not for a desirous thought? Gross and subtle thought determines emotions. Nonattachment to thought reduces emotional reactivity.

Renunciation, meditation, and compassion are necessary if we are to reduce the potency of thoughts. A genuine practitioner skillfully and unceasingly integrates these three components together. But in order to do this, you must understand what they are. If you are completely caught up in the *idea* of renunciation and meanwhile mistreat your partner, saying, "It is because of you that I am caught in samsara!" then you have missed the point. You are here because of your attachment. You mistreat your partner because of attachment.

Sometimes I feel as though many of us do not know how to balance these teachings. One day I will die, and I can't take my family with me. I cannot, as the Chinese emperors or Egyptian pharaohs of the past thought, carry my wife and possessions into the afterlife. When I think about death, renunciation naturally happens. I don't like to think about the fact that I will *naturally* detach from all that I have accumulated in this world, but what to do? If it is the way things actually are, we have to think about it.

When you try to change too much of the Buddha's teaching to fit your current worldview, then your habits don't change. Sometimes the Buddha's teachings are not so nice to hear, but that is the point! The Buddha's teachings may be displeasing if your current way of living and set of values reflect a mistaken understanding of what brings happiness. When I go to the doctor and he tells me I need to eat healthier food, I don't like it! I try to *reinterpret* what he says. My reinterpretation doesn't hurt the doctor; it hurts me. For the same reason, we must not reinterpret Dharma teachings too liberally. The purpose of practice is not only to achieve happiness in this lifetime but also to gain fearlessness in the face of death.

We do not know what is going to happen when we die. Although we may contemplate the possibility or validity of reincarnation, unless we are very realized we cannot know for sure whether we will have a future rebirth or not. The problem with assuming it all ends at death is that we tend to indulge in damaging behaviors and patterns. If you pay attention to fellow Buddhists, you will see that those practitioners who have a stronger conviction in rebirth are usually more mindful and skillful than those who do not. They are more cautious with their physical and verbal actions. They assume that the consequences of their every action will come back around. Ironically, as a result of such attention to karma, they are actually freer. We do not believe in "punishment" in Buddhism, but we do recognize that every action has a consequence and that anything we experience now is the result of previous actions. That is the law of karmic result.

When we start to interpret the teachings of the Dharma in abstract ways, we inevitably diminish the potency of the law of cause and effect. Every practice offered by the Buddha is layered with meaning, and we should get to the heart of that meaning even if it is not what we want to hear. In the sutras, we come across stories of monks going out on alms walks. When they hear how monks "beg," people come to think that Buddhism advocates poverty or that monks receive their food by the grace of God and surrender to Divine Will. This understanding is a superimposition. The monks are actually inviting people to share in the merit of the Dharma, inviting the community to practice generosity and connect with the monks' virtuous activities. We can only understand this kind of detail when we make the effort to study. So let's not just rely upon our ideas of how things are but actually get to the meaning of things.

A monk or nun should not be judgmental when accepting alms. They cannot say, "I like this and I don't like that. I won't accept this food that you are giving me because you didn't cook it well." The Buddha explained the benefits of accepting alms without discrimination. We reduce our desire and judgment. We have correct discipline. We do not engage in unnecessary debate. We do not praise ourselves or criticize others. Our attachment decreases. We check our anger. We reduce our material concerns. Just as the meaning of the practice of receiving alms is not immediately apparent, the benefit of renunciation on all levels will only in time be brought fully to light.

Cultivating Renunciation

Consider the following five questions slowly and honestly. Spend at least one or two minutes on each question, examining what arises for you as you proceed.

- How strong is my practice of renunciation? In other words, how much do I cling to a sense of self?

- What is my motivation for most things? How selfish am I?

- How undistracted am I during formal meditation?

- How mindful am I in my actions?

- How attached am I to the result of my practice?

In addition to contemplating these questions, throughout your day, examine which of the eight worldly concerns are strongest for you. The eight worldly concerns are:

1. Seeking gain
2. Fearing loss
3. Desiring pleasure
4. Opposing displeasure

5. Enjoying praise
6. Disliking blame
7. Coveting happiness
8. Avoiding suffering

Knowing where you are susceptible, exercise mindfulness and guard against the eight worldly concerns.

Remember that the Buddha's teaching on renunciation is a form of self-compassion. Renunciation is how we become free.

4
Loving-Kindness, Compassion, Joy, Equanimity

1st: Loving-Kindness

The wise will abide in loving-kindness.
They remain within pure compassion, forever equal-minded
toward enjoyments and the whole of existence.
Cultivating samadhi, they will attain awakening.

—CHAPTER 9

WE ALL POSSESS the seed of kindness, the seed of caring. Even the most afflicted have this seed. When I first began to practice loving-kindness and compassion, my seed was small, but as I watered it, it began to sprout. Then, although the sprout was there, even with a lot of training it wasn't turning into a tree. This was because I could not see everybody equally. My compassion, my caring and love, did not spread to everyone in the same way.

It can be challenging when we begin to develop the four immeasurables of loving-kindness, compassion, joy, and equanimity. As we cultivate these mind states, we see where we are stuck. Yet when we grow these qualities and embrace them through the profound view of emptiness, we enter the Great Vehicle. These mind states, which characterize aspirational bodhichitta, turn us toward virtue and become a source of joy for everyone with whom we are connected.

> You who thoroughly cultivated loving-kindness
> are the spiritual guide of all beings.
> Unshakeable like Mount Meru,
> you remain utterly unperturbed.
>
> —CHAPTER 14

When the Buddha sat beneath the Bodhi Tree and the hordes of demons, known as maras, rose up around him, hurling spears and shooting arrows, his samadhi transformed the weapons into a rain of blossoms. Loving-kindness has the power to turn enemies into teachers and aggressions into adornments. It is the ground from which the other three immeasurables draw their power. When we train in loving-kindness, we expand outward into the experience of those around us. Our tightness loosens, our compassion grows. We feel the joys and sufferings of others more deeply, and we are moved to help them. We take delight in the successes of our friends. Our equanimity becomes rooted in an indestructibly pure intention, in which distance and closeness of relation are no longer relevant. This is why the Buddha said we can become unshakeable like Mount Meru. We become warm and unmovable.

Those who abide in loving-kindness and have
    no anger
will have no difficulty in obtaining this samadhi.

—CHAPTER 2

First, we try to generate a sense of warmth for someone close to our heart. We begin with our child or our mother, or even our family pet. By turning our mind toward that dear one, love arises naturally. Whether or not we see it now, our very nature is filled with this supreme love. Because our nature is endowed with love, we don't need to be afraid that we lack the capacity to feel love. We can start to generate a warm heart by reminding ourselves to reduce our selfish motivations.

If you try to cultivate love without giving up your hidden agendas, it is like building a house of cards. Attachment and expectation undo us. These expressions of self-centered motivation quietly pull out cards from the foundation, causing our whole house of practice to collapse. We have to do away with any sort of expectation of reward for the love we cultivate. Love itself must become the source of our joy. If you practice with a loved one first, without agenda or expectation for yourself, you can slowly build a solid foundation.

In order to practice loving-kindness in this way, recall the face of a loved one. While bringing up a sense of care and warmth for that person, earnestly think, "I don't want any self-gain from this practice. I don't want any respect from this person or for them even to develop a positive opinion of me. I don't want anything from this person. I don't want anything from this person, not a single grain. Everything is impermanent—anything I gain will not solve my problems anyway." Think like this and turn your mind toward this person, wishing them to be free from all suffering. Make the aspiration that they will experience unshakeable happiness and tenderness of heart.

As this cultivation becomes stronger and our love more pronounced, we begin to express it more fluidly to others. We become more deeply attuned and loving to our friends and family, and our love also flows to people we've just met. Slowly, it reaches many beings, and then, all beings. The expansiveness of a mind abiding in such a love is inconceivable. As the Buddha said, this type of love makes it very easy to obtain the ultimate samadhi. It leads us out of our obsessions and into the supremely blissful view.

2ND: COMPASSION

You see how beings delight in their projections
and you see their suffering.
Therefore, you teach them emptiness,
profundity, peace, and nonconceptuality.
                                    —CHAPTER 14

The Buddha says we are naturally saddened when we see how sentient beings delight in illusory projections. We see how suffering arises when family, friends, and others fall into thoughts and expectations that are total illusions.

Every single person is caught up in a web of their own projections, and because of this every person suffers.

Some of us think, "How can I have compassion for all beings?" or "There are beings I see who do not appear to be suffering. How can I have compassion for them?" It might seem impossible, but we do learn how to relate to everyone's suffering. We start by acknowledging the great delusion of the mind's projections.

Honestly speaking, on the relative level we are all different. Financially, physically, on the mental level, the emotional level, on almost *every* level, we can see clear differences between people. If we focus on the differences, compassion won't blossom fully. You might think, "This person looks much happier than I am, so why should I practice compassion toward her?" But if we practice in this way, we base our practice on projection.

Projection is not a reliable basis for generating a caring attitude toward another person, for it is inevitably tied to judgment. "Our education is so different—how can I relate to you and your worldview? How can I relate to your outlook when we are so different?" First, we relate to our own ego and our own self-focused attitudes, and we come to understand how these attitudes cause our personal suffering. When we intimately understand the patterns of our own ego, it becomes easier to empathize with the way the critical thoughts of others cause them to suffer.

I once suspected that if I trained in compassion I would lose something, some sort of confidence or machismo. I believed that someone who possesses great compassion has a hard time saying "no." I was worried I wouldn't keep my strength, that my compassion practice would motivate me to say "yes" at compromising times, and that I would lose dignity.

This view arises in the early stages of compassion practice, because we are still self-centered. We are so conditioned to acquire and to protect things that when we try to practice compassion for others, we are actually motivated by our own self-interest. We know that generating compassion is a good thing and that it feels good, that it is *right*. So we cultivate it in order to do what is right. This is known as *compassion with agenda*.

When we have compassion or kindness with such an attitude, we find that when people don't respond to our compassion in the way we expect, we become angry. I was recently walking in New York City, and I came upon a homeless man lying in a pile of dirty blankets beneath a concrete overhang near a grocery store. Seeing him, I was motivated to go into the store to look for something I could give to him. There were three metal pots of soup, and I examined them to see which was the warmest and smelled the most delicious. I ladled out a nice big cup, purchased it, and walked out onto the street. Very gently, I bent over and offered it to him. He looked at me and said, "I don't want it." I said, "I just bought this for you, it's fresh." He said, "I don't want it!" In the past I may have been upset by his reaction; after all, I just bought a New York–priced bowl of soup for the man. But this time I was able to say, "Okay," walk two blocks, and offer it to another homeless man. If I had been angry with the first man, it would have revealed to me that my compassion practice was still very much with an agenda.

We can check for agenda in the simplest of compassionate acts. For example, oftentimes we try to be warm and friendly, and we extend a smile to someone who then frowns in response. If we become upset, we can see the extent of our agenda, and then work with this condition.

I am not saying you should viciously judge yourself as you cultivate compassion. I am saying we need to notice what kind of behavior we have. We don't need self-judgment, but we do need self-awareness. We actually need to develop a pattern of nonjudgment. In the past, I found I could be quite self-centered—judging myself in this way and that way. I have trained to see the intricacies of that attitude and have begun to see that everyone else has these tendencies as well. The way I obsess over myself is exactly how others obsess over themselves. These tendencies are nothing new; they are exactly what the Buddha taught about. Recognizing the intricacies of self-centeredness is the first step toward true compassion.

We usually have no wish to be free of this pattern of self-obsession. Some great masters have said that if we really understand what compassion is, if we know the complexities, intricacies, and simplicity of the practice, then there is nothing else to develop.

Let us not get stuck in the warm feelings that arise when we begin to practice compassion. Sometimes we comfort someone in a time of trouble and say, "It's okay," or

"Everything's fine." We might take a cursory look into our motivation and come to the conclusion that we have no attachment. We feel delighted.

But say someone comes to you, someone you don't necessarily like, and asks you for assistance. You might be able to generate a sense of warmth for this person, but you are hesitant to put compassion into action. You might feel lazy, or find something else you have to do, even with a faint sense of well-wishing in your heart. This, my dear, is *cheating*! You're staying within mental compassion but you're not getting down to the heart of the matter, down to the real ground. When we notice this happening, we need to ask ourselves, "What am I really missing here? What do I need to do to really improve?"

I started to ask myself, "What is the key to compassion?" Through greater and greater familiarization, I discovered that the only time I can have pure compassion is when I am free from ego. This is what the Buddha refers to in the *King of Meditation Sutra* when he says, "Therefore, you teach them emptiness, profundity, peace, and nonconceptuality."

The profound equality of all beings is known only in the moment in which the "I" no longer exists. Only through the recognition of emptiness is there stainless compassion. This stainless compassion, inseparable from emptiness, is none other than the ultimate samadhi.

> Youthful Moon, what is the clear demonstration of samadhi? Nonconceptual; intentionless; birthless; ceaseless; without reference point; without men-

tal engagement; the full extinction of perception;
the ground that is free from afflictive emotions; the
peaceful ground that eliminates all elaborations;
the training of all the bodhisattvas; the domain of
all the tathagatas; the perfection of all qualities:
this is called the clear demonstration of samadhi,
Youth. Bodhisattva mahasattvas who abide by this
clear demonstration of samadhi are never separated from samadhi. Their minds are not confused.
They have great compassion and benefit beings in
immeasurable ways.

—CHAPTER 13

The point is that the highest compassion is actually completely nonconceptual; it is indivisible from the highest
insight. As soon as I think, "Put compassion into action,"
the pure moment of compassion is gone because thinking
has taken over. This is why pure compassion arises from
the genuine meditation in which thoughts about "you and
me" cannot get in the way. We will learn how to develop this
egoless meditation later in the text.

Now the question is, how can you bring this compassion,
this emptiness meditation, into your daily life? Slowly,
slowly. The best way to do this is to alternate between generating compassion and enhancing your realization of
emptiness. By first practicing conceptual compassion con-
sistently for those around you, and then eventually com-
bining that compassionate aspiration with the meditation
practice that is free from self and other, a day will come

when a moment of pure, egoless compassion arises. That will be the happiest day of your life.

Practicing real compassion with release from ego is like dealing with a scale that has been piled with weights on one side. One by one, you remove each weight of grasping, agenda, and attachment. For instance, "This person mistreated me"—let go, remove that weight. "I'm going to have compassion for this person but not for that person"—let go, remove that weight. "This person didn't respond well to my compassion and my offer of help"—remove that weight and let go.

Compassion is the mirror. Compassion indicates whether you have realized your nature or not. It is a sign. If your compassion is self-centered, if it reveals a self-centered agenda, then you are currently self-centered. If you experience the warmth of compassion but it is suffused with a sense of superiority, this means you are proud. If your compassion demands some sort of response from someone, it means you have attachment.

There is also weak compassion. I am not referring to the strength of the feeling but to an absence of dignity. Here, dignity means knowing that your very nature is compassionate. Perhaps you see an injured dog and you say, "Oh poor dog, I cannot do anything for you. Oh, how I hate these people who mistreated this dog. I am going to report them to animal services." In your indignation you feel justified, validated, and righteous. When we are engaged in truly dignified compassion, feelings of justification, validation, and righteousness are not present. Actions suffused with these feelings appear to be strong, but they actually constitute a weaker compassion because they are motivated by strong feelings of attachment to a particular ethic, which naturally invites aversion and distaste for those who do not hold that ethic. Dignified compassion comes from recognizing the intrinsic goodness of every being. Someone who has this compassion does not fall into the duality of demonizing some and glorifying others but takes confident action with awareness and love.

Here is another example involving a mistreated animal. Once I watched a show on television about a man in Los Angeles who adopted a neglected dog. He said he connected to the dog's suffering because he himself was abandoned at thirteen years old. His emotional response to the dog was based in his own history. He gave rise to compassion because he could empathize with the suffering of being neglected. It is good that he was able to generate compassion for the dog, but imagine if he developed that feeling of care more fully. Through understanding that everyone experiences suffering, his compassion would stream forth beyond this situational empathy to include all beings. Imagine if his compassion emerged completely unconditioned and uninhibited, free from clinging to own's own experience.

We read in the texts that compassion means wishing all beings to be free from suffering and the cause of suffering. We sometimes generate this feeling or make this aspiration, and then just leave it at that. But if you realize self-lessness, your compassion reflects this realization, and its expression becomes completely unstained by any clinging to self and other, completely free from any thought of who does and does not deserve compassion.

When we become this compassion, we effortlessly teach this compassion. Even our bodies become an expression of its impartiality. An awakened being who is an expression of compassion cannot fit within the walls of any projection. They naturally teach profundity, peace, and inconceivability.

3RD: JOY

All these beings are my kin.
I rejoice in whatever merit they have,
three times by day and three by night,
setting the mind upon awakening.
I rejoice in the purest discipline
of those who commit no wrong,
even at the cost of their own lives.
I rejoice in whatever merit
is in the excellent aspirations of bodhisattvas.
I rejoice in those who have faith in the Buddha,
and likewise in the Dharma and the Sangha.
I rejoice in those who make offerings to the tathagatas
out of their intense desire to reach awakening.

—CHAPTER 26

It is so powerful to intentionally rejoice in the goodness of others. When we take joy in the actions of those working toward supreme awakening, we ourselves rapidly move along the path. The Buddha said that in order to practice rejoicing we have to see all sentient beings as our loved ones. It is so simple and intuitive.

If I am a pessimistic person when working with my students on a problem, I can get tired and dragged down from complaining about the issue rather than finding ways to solve it. If you are focused on the negative, you start breathing heavily, you notice shoulder or back pain, and you still have all of your work to do. It can get very messy.

When you train in taking joy and are able to bring the recognition of emptiness into your experience, you start to eliminate the suction of negativity. So please train in seeing the positive qualities in your life. If it is snowing, don't focus on the dirty streets and your limited mobility. Notice the enlivening breeze. Contemplate where it comes from, all the people it will touch. When it is raining, don't focus on the wet and cold. Notice how the leaves become vivid with raindrops and see the branches swaying. This is how you can change your mindset.

If you have a problem, you don't need to shout at yourself to fix it. Speak to yourself with a small smile. Ask, "What is my problem today?" A small smile helps a lot. You should not be too self-focused. This diminishes happiness. It's one of our fundamental issues. It prevents us from taking delight in the successes of others, and it sucks away our joy.

Imagine you see two people laughing together in the park. It is a balmy summer evening and the weather is perfect. The sunset lights up their lovely red picnic blanket, they are sharing good food, fireflies are starting to come alive. But you have a problem with your own spouse. You see a couple, maybe kissing, and you get angry. You think to yourself, "Why do they have to kiss in front of everyone? Get a room!"

Why do we have to be angry when we see something like this? It's such a self-focused reaction. Why can't we rejoice for them and think, "I am so happy for you!" This would be a skillful way to take advantage of this situation. In the moment of rejoicing, their happiness becomes our happiness too. However, we should not think, "I wish that were me." That would also be self-focused. Take delight in their happiness and it naturally becomes yours.

The root of virtue is a mind free from the three poisons of aversion, attachment, and ignorance. The root of merit is the practice of the six perfections (in Sanskrit they are known as the *paramitas*). They constitute engaged bodhichitta. The first five—generosity, discipline, patience, diligence, and meditation—are the source of merit. When they are embraced by the sixth—transcendent wisdom (*prajna-paramita*)—they become true paramitas, or perfections. A virtuous mind that practices the paramitas is suffused with supreme joy; and this is the mind of a bodhisattva.

Taking joy and finding inspiration in the minds of the bodhisattvas creates a virtuous impact on our lives and on the lives of those around us. Rejoicing in the goodness of everyone reduces jealousy and produces faith in the practice. Furthermore, when you rejoice in others who have confidence in the teachings, this enhances your own relationship with the Dharma and the noble ones, the bodhisattvas. When you rejoice in your Dharma friends who are doing positive actions, like making offerings, you also acquire the merit of their actions.

To dedicate your merit to the awakening of all beings is the ultimate act of rejoicing. When you think, "May all of this action lead to the temporary and ultimate benefit of everyone," you are actually rejoicing in the happiness of infinite beings. To adopt such a mindset is to create the condition for the arising of qualities in you and in others.

4TH: EQUANIMITY

Youth, consider this: If they are endowed with this one Dharma, bodhisattva mahasattvas will attain these qualities and swiftly, perfectly realize unsurpassable, authentic, and complete awakening. What is this one Dharma? Youth, bodhisattva mahasattvas regard all beings equally. Their minds are beneficent, without anger or partiality.

—CHAPTER 1

Equanimity is not a frozen state. It is not a mind of a stone. Equanimity is at root a loving mind. It is the flexibility that arises on the basis of seeing everyone equally. It embraces the other practices of the immeasurables. Although it is sometimes listed last in texts on the four immeasurables, equanimity often comes first in the oral instructions because it is the foundation from which the other three can fully expand.

Equanimity can be separated into three different levels. The first level of equanimity is to see all sentient beings with an equal amount of love. Buddhists understand that we have many lifetimes of connection with every being. We nurture this understanding to the point that it arises in our experience, and eventually we can walk in the world with it.

The second level of equanimity relates to our nature. We see that all beings share the same essence—the essence of the Buddha. That is, we recall that we all have Buddha-nature. At the same time, we see that beings are ignorant of their Buddha-nature and are therefore stuck in samsara.

The final, genuine equanimity is to be free from both concepts of equal and unequal. Such freedom brings supreme flexibility. When this happens, we have no clinging to ideas, we have no judgment, we can't even cling to the "view." In other words, we cannot obsess. Still, we are lucidly awake. The essence of equanimity is to be incapable of clinging to anything. In the absence of clinging, there is so much love and understanding. From this place, our compassion completely unfolds. It naturally becomes as vast as space.

Cultivating the Four Immeasurables

1. Spend five to ten minutes cultivating the four immeasurables by quietly repeating the following aspiration:

> May all beings have happiness and the cause
> of happiness;
> May they be free from suffering and the cause
> of suffering;
> May they never be separate from the supreme
> happiness devoid of suffering;
> May they remain in boundless equanimity,
> beyond attachment and aversion to those
> near and far.

Connect with the meaning of these words. Radiate loving-kindness and compassion out to every being, excluding no one. Take care to not overexert and "squeeze" your mind to try and generate love.

2. Once you have cultivated the four immeasurables for some time, add this phrase to the end of the first aspiration:

> Wherever space pervades, all sentient beings
> are my loved ones. They have suffering and the
> cause of suffering. May they become free from
> suffering and realize the enlightenment of total
> awakening.

3. Throughout your day actively rejoice in the successes of others. Again and again, rejoice in the practice and the accomplishments of the buddhas and bodhisattvas.

4. Nurture the understanding that throughout infinite lifetimes of connection, all beings have been our mothers. With a love that extends to everyone equally, recall that we all have Buddha-nature. Again and again, recall that everyone has Buddha-nature. When this recollection becomes strong, direct, and authentic, concept-free equanimity will unfold.

5
ASKING THE BUDDHA TO STAY

The bodhisattva mahasattva Maitreya made mental prostrations to the Buddha and mentally circumambulated him three times. Then, leaving the congregation, he traveled to the great stupa at Vulture Peak, the King of Mountains, sacred site of countless buddhas, numerous as the grains of sand in the ocean. There, for the Victorious One's enjoyment, he blessed Vulture Peak so that it instantly became a level, open space with no sticks, thorns, stones, pebbles, or gravel, and the entire surrounding area was transformed into the seven precious substances.

—CHAPTER 17

MAYBE YOU ALREADY have some compassion, are practicing right action, have some knowledge and some experience in meditation. Once this has happened, you start to move from mere technical training into what we can call the "spiritual aspect" of the method. From this point, you will only advance quickly if you have spiritual support, if you aren't spiritually lonely, and if you have spiritual confidence.

1ST: GAIN SPIRITUAL SUPPORT

You gain spiritual support by relying on the realization of those who came before you. You cannot walk this whole path alone, and if you try, you will fail. So, you begin to turn your mind toward the Buddha and all those who inherited the teachings of the Buddha, all the great masters of the past.

Maitreya's actions in the above quotation from the *King of Meditation Sutra* are not just storytelling—his activity shows us how to practice. It is due to the power of the Buddha that Maitreya was able to bless the land for the Buddha's enjoyment. This is a very profound point. Through prostration, circumambulation, and supplication he was able to connect with the wisdom of the Buddha and thereby bless the earth through that wisdom.

Prostration is an ancient way of demonstrating respect in many cultures and traditions, and the practice of circumambulating representations of the Buddha's body, speech, and mind dates back to the time of Buddha himself. When Maitreya paid homage through prostration and circumambulation, the Buddha blessed his mind to be able to experience the world in a pure way. Maitreya saw the top of Vulture Peak as adorned with sparkling jewels. The air smelled sweet and delicious, the ground was exceptionally flat and even. It was as though a billionaire had organized the land for his daughter's wedding. Nothing was left unadorned, rough, or imperfect. Everything was exceptional, pushing the limits of splendor.

Whatever we imagine will produce how we feel, and our feelings have an impact on the people surrounding us. When I walk into a room full of people who are angry, I can feel that anger—it is expressed to me in countless subtle ways. Likewise, the inconceivably powerful mind of an awakened being has the power to engender experiences that accord with love and wisdom, and we call these "blessings." Through the power of the Buddha's samadhi and Maitreya's training and receptiveness, the land became beautiful in Maitreya's actual experience.

2ND: DISPEL SPIRITUAL LONELINESS

You can practice in the same way as Maitreya by visualizing all the loving awakened beings in front of you. They are here for one purpose and one purpose only: to help you. The sky is not large enough to hold so many radiant bodies. Cultivate the certainty that golden Shakyamuni Buddha and all of those who have gone beyond samsara are with you, from now until enlightenment. Their presence says, "Don't worry about the small stuff." You should think that any obstacles you may have are just peanuts for them. Connecting with this feeling of being buoyed up by the wisdom of countless victorious meditators is what is known as spiritual support.

Look at your practice when you don't train in this way, when you don't have any spiritual support, when you don't have awakened beings to go to for refuge. Look at your experience when you don't supplicate. If you meditate without any of this then you feel quite lonely. Without support, you may have this hidden but strong suspicion that you will fail to attain the ultimate fruit of the path. You know you can succeed in some meditation and that it can benefit you a little, but the goal of enlightenment is usually well beyond the scope of what you believe is possible. Maybe you can become a little happier—but, enlightenment? Come on!

Spiritual loneliness is mentioned in the teachings of the Foundational Vehicle, but not very extensively. The Mahayana emphasizes it further, and in the Vajrayana it becomes extremely important. When we begin meditation practice in the presence of all the loving buddhas of all genders, all of them, surrounding us and actually looking at us, their presence and their eyes serve to remind us, "If you fail now, that's all right. Do it anyway."

To completely unveil our wisdom, this kind of total love and nonjudgmental compassion needs to saturate us. "If I fail now, fine!" When we have this confidence, we never feel alone. I gave this instruction to a group of people who don't usually practice in such a way. I asked them, "Do you feel lonely when you do meditation?" It is true that they take refuge in the Buddha and chant his name, but they never chant with the thought that every buddha is present—every single buddha, male and female, red and yellow, big and small, from the past and the present and the future. I told them that if you meditate, visualizing you are in front of countless buddhas who blaze like the sun and direct their minds of wisdom toward you, then you don't really need to do anything else. You just sit there and meditation comes.

At some pilgrimage places, meditation comes automatically. You don't have to put great effort into the practice. If you go to Bodhgaya, the place where Buddha attained enlightenment, you have probably experienced this effortless meditation. The conditions are so conducive to practice that one just enters into a natural flow of meditation. This experience of naturally contacting wisdom is known as "receiving blessings." People travel the world to receive blessings from holy places and holy beings. They trek over mountains and endure hardships to receive blessings. Blessings arise through the power of great meditators and the spaces and objects connected with those practitioners. Once you have received blessings, you can take them with you wherever you go. Simply think, "I have the blessings with me now." Sit in your room and think, "I am in Bodhgaya and the Buddha is in front of me right now." Burn incense or light a candle as an offering and sit in the presence of the Buddha. Through inviting blessings, we are not lonely and we enhance our practice. We become more concerned with blessings when we want to swim down deep into wisdom, rather than just learn meditation.

Many people ask, "Why visualize the Buddha?" It's actually quite straightforward. If I want to learn how to build a nuclear reactor, I am fairly certain I will visualize the presence of Einstein. I will think, "Einstein, please bless me to become a physicist like you." My mind will turn toward Einstein's qualities. I will align my experience with the quality of his intelligence. Through recollecting him, I will reflect on his qualities, which will impress upon my own mind.

Similarly, when I visualize my grandmother, a particular feeling comes, which is her specific love and care, that is then engendered within me.

Something similar takes place when we visualize the Buddha, though there is an added dimension and result. Visualizing the Buddha is particularly potent because the wisdom of the Buddha is already ever-present. We connect to the unobstructed wisdom mind of the Buddha through first connecting to his form. The power of this type of recollection and subsequent connection cannot be overstated. Something extraordinary begins to happen when we recollect the Buddha rather than an ordinary being.

The Buddha taught the genuine practice of meditation. He taught the path which leads to freedom from ego-clinging and desire. The Buddha taught the methods that will lead us to freedom. If we want to gain these methods, we ask the Buddha to bless us. We don't ask him to bless us with a million dollars or to make us like Bill Gates or the president of the United States, but rather that we may swiftly gain his realization.

I used to encounter difficulties when I meditated because my mind did not listen to my commands. When I encountered a difficulty in my practice, it did not mean my mind was bad. It just meant my mind could not listen. Do you know why that was? I had spoiled my mind. Throughout my life I had told my mind, "Do whatever you want." Then when I began to sit and meditate, my mind would naturally just do whatever it wanted.

When the thought arises, "I don't like meditating," we

need to return to the practice at hand. Eventually, when the mind starts to think, "I love everybody, and I love to meditate," and we are experiencing waves of bliss, we also return to the practice at hand. "It's okay," we tell our mind, and this becomes a powerful tool in our meditation arsenal.

"I am hungry."

"It's okay, go back to meditation."

"I am tired, and I need a nap."

"It's okay, for a little while, go back to meditation."

This is not to say we should not attend to our bodies—of course we must be healthy and rested. The point here is that as we continue to walk the path, the mind will not support us. Through practice we try to soften the mind, to make it malleable, and eventually undermine it. The mind doesn't want to be undermined, of course, and it shows its resistance right from the beginning. I think you all know the result of a spoiled mind: stress, exhaustion, anger, fear, and all the other negative states that generally lead us to inquire about meditation in the first place. Whatever difficulty we have with practice, it is produced by our mind. When we supplicate the buddhas and bodhisattvas, we are calling for the intervention of wisdom, which cannot be tainted or swayed or corrupted by mind. We invoke the wisdom that burns away the cranky mind.

Somebody once told me that she practices forgiveness. I said, "Don't try to practice forgiveness." "What! Why not?" she exclaimed. What we are learning to do is to forget. When you forgive, the problem is your train of thought, which goes, "I forgive you for what you've done." You are reminding yourself that somebody did something to you. I am not telling you to suppress, I'm saying that clinging to a narrative of forgiveness always reminds us of a "wrong." When we are reminded, we hold on. The best place to get to is "Oh really? I already forgot about the whole thing!" Then there is no need for forgiveness, because you have already released the wrong. You don't carry a stone in your heart.

If you can do this, then it means you are not holding on to the past. It means you are not attached to the dualistic narrative of harm. It means you do not go back in time. You do not internalize the sense of being a victim. On the other hand, by clinging to forgiveness, you keep the source of your pain, the source of your attachment, while trying to cover it up through the idea that "I," as a solid unconditioned entity, am forgiving "you," another permanent substantial being. How can we find release if we do this?

We approach confession in a similar way in Buddhist practice. Ordinarily, when confessing, we hold on to the very action for which we feel remorse. We should confess in the same way that we quickly and firmly slam a hand down upon a table.

"I confess." Bam!

We confess, and then we decisively let go. We gain certainty in the purifying power of confession by gaining confidence in the presence and love of the buddhas. This comes through the continuous receiving of blessings. We receive blessings with the same decisiveness with which we confess.

"I have received the blessings." Bam! Let go!

In the Vajrayana, for example, we often practice relating to Buddha Vajrasattva, who is the embodiment of pure wisdom. We imagine brilliant light rays streaming forth from Vajrasattva's heart, carrying splendid offerings to all the buddhas and gathering their blessings, which then stream back to Vajrasattva. Receiving these light rays, Vajrasattva blazes with wisdom light. We then ask him to purify all of our negative karma. Vajrasattva, looking upon us, says, "Yes, you are purified," and we actually have the experience of being purified. As we practice this again and again, we actually give rise to the experience of total purity, and our actions, speech, and mentality begin to reflect that. The entire practice takes place in the mind, but it begets a truly transformative result.

The practices of mentally inviting a buddha to abide, mentally prostrating to him, and mentally making offerings all come from the Mahayana sutras. Those of us who practice the Vajrayana should know that many of our methods come from the Mahayana. The methods of the Vajrayana are not something that Vajrayana teachers created out of nowhere. Like Maitreya, we should ask the Buddha to bless our minds and our places of practice. When we do this, we are following in the footsteps of the bodhisattvas in the *King of Meditation Sutra.*

3RD: DEVELOP SPIRITUAL CONFIDENCE

Thus, remember Buddha as the embodiment
and immeasurable wisdom of the victorious ones.

If you constantly cultivate this recollection,
your mind will truly settle on it.

—CHAPTER 4

I have a friend who seemingly does the practice of visualizing the buddhas in exactly the way I do, yet whenever I ask him if he receives the blessings he says no.

"How are you today?" I ask. "How is your meditation?"

"My meditation is okay."

"Did you receive the blessings?"

"Um, no. Well, I'm not sure."

He always says the same thing. Then he asks me, "Did you receive the blessings?"

I always respond, "Yes, I did receive the blessings."

It is our pattern. Whenever I ask him if he received the blessings and he says, "I'm not sure," it is precisely this uncertainty, this "I'm not sure," that obstructs him from being blessed.

I receive the blessings because I am in the habit of thinking that I do. I have confidence in this and do my best to turn my mind toward the ever-present buddhas and bodhisattvas. This man never receives the blessings because he is habituated to the thought that he does not receive them. Being in the habit of receiving blessings is spiritual confidence. Slowly, slowly, we grow the confidence that we are immersed in the loving-kindness and compassion of awakened mind, steeped in the support of buddhas and bodhisattvas. This is not a blind type of confidence; rather it arises from the undeniable experience of being saturated with love and wisdom.

This confidence is free from pride because it does not produce judgment; it does not widen the gap between self and other. As we develop this confidence we practice compassion, we watch our judgment, and we do not reify the narrative, "Oh, I received blessings and therefore I am a superior practitioner." It's not like that.

Through the course of my training, I have occasionally felt I am not receiving the blessings. When this happens, I have to immediately change my mind. I have to instantly think, "I *did* receive the blessings." This is very important. It is how we train in the spiritual aspect of the path. It is very different from the technical aspects of the path, which involve the parsing of experience, the method of meditation, and looking quite analytically at the mind.

The spiritual aspect is also method, but it leans away from how we conventionally understand method. We need both the spiritual and the technical aspects of method. When we combine them, we have totally firm confidence in the Dharma. If you take out the spiritual aspect, the motivation driving the technical aspect does not last very long. And if you have the spiritual aspect without the technical aspect, then Buddhism becomes blind faith.

Inviting the Buddha's Blessing

- Prepare a shrine with representations of the enlightened body, speech, and mind. For example, your practice place could have a statue (body), a scripture (speech), and a stupa (mind).

- Sit upright but at ease upon your meditation seat.

- Generate the sense that wisdom of the Buddha is ever-present and ask the Buddha to bless your place of practice.

- Generate a strong sense of conviction that you receive the blessings.

- Remember you are receiving the blessings in order to tame the negative emotions of the mind, to transform the mind from ego-clinging to egolessness, and to realize the very nature of the mind.

6
OFFERING FOR BLISS

1ST: GIVE WITH BODY AND SPEECH

When striving for this samadhi,
there is no neglecting offering to the
victorious ones.

—CHAPTER 2

W HEN I WAS visiting Burma, I went to a place where ancient practitioners had built beautiful stupas. I could see amazing gems—diamonds, deep green emeralds, and flaming rubies—encrusting the tops of the stupas. From a certain vantage point, the gems glittered and sparkled in the sun. Burma is known for its gems, and I'm fairly sure that practitioners pulled those rubies and diamonds from their own land and placed them in these representations of enlightened mind.

Around the stupa complex there were shops where I could buy gold leaf and offer it on the stupa walls. My family and I were invited to adorn and beautify the stupas. People in the marketplace sold lamps for offering, and the custodians would leave them burning all night. Seeing an opportunity to make merit, or "assemble the conditions that lead to awakening," my immediate thought was "Okay, I must sponsor these offerings right now." As soon as I began to purchase the offerings, my in-laws decided they wanted to make offerings as well.

Two days later, we paid a visit to another Burmese monastery. The dollar exchange rate was strong; one hundred U.S. dollars at the exchange booth would get me ninety-thousand Burmese kyat. I exchanged a couple hundred dollars and they gave me a huge bag of money. I felt so wealthy.

In Burma, it's quite inexpensive to live and food does not cost very much, even for poor people. I turned to my father in-law and told him I wanted to go to a local monastery to practice generosity. So, I went to the monastery with my wife and daughter, who was very young at the time, and a few others. We placed our bundles of money on the offering plate—these big, thick stacks of cash—and everybody bowed to the image of the Buddha. I know how to bow Burmese style, so rather than bowing in the way that I traditionally learned, I bowed in the Burmese style out of respect. The rest of my family members and friends bowed in the Tibetan style. A friend turned to me with a smile on his face and said, "How do you know how to bow like that?" And I said, "You just need to observe!"

In order to show respect, we need to be very careful in our observations. The people taking care of the Burmese monastery were delighted to see me bow in their style. Momentarily changing the manner in which I bowed was in itself an offering. We can be generous with our respect continuously. In that moment, I was able to see the value in practicing generosity and seize the opportunity to align my mind with virtue. We need to know how to harvest our opportunities for giving. These opportunities to give rarely just come out of nowhere. We must actually stand up and create them, and when the moment is upon us, we have to give as much as we can. It has become so clear to me that through generosity we fulfill our worldly wishes more quickly, and our practice becomes smoother.

In the *King of Meditation Sutra,* the Buddha recounts one of his previous lives, long before he took birth as Siddhartha Gautama. In that life, he was the student of an ancient buddha, and in the presence of that buddha he made many offerings and prayers of aspiration. The merit generated by those offerings became the force that propelled him toward his eventual realization. It is also said that Shakyamuni Buddha praised the names of eighty previous buddhas to whom he had made offerings over the course of two eons.

When we offer praise to the Buddha, we are engaging in a type of mindfulness. We recall the qualities that are present within our own true nature. By recalling those qualities, we immediately begin the process of revealing them. When we praise the Buddha, realization becomes desirable, inspiring. When we praise the Buddha, we place value in the attainment of the truth, and thus gain tremendous merit. The *King of Meditation Sutra* teaches us how to praise the buddhas by reflecting on their qualities.

The Tathagata is in accord with all merit. He does not waste the roots of virtue. Patience is his ornament. He is the foundation of the treasures of merit. He is adorned with the minor marks. He blossoms with the flowers of the major marks. His activity is timely and appropriate. When one sees him, he is without disharmony. He brings true joy to those who long with faith. His knowledge cannot be overpowered. His strengths cannot be challenged. He is the teacher of all sentient beings. He is the father of bodhisattvas. He is the king of noble ones. He is the guide of those who just set out on the path. He possesses immeasurable wisdom. He possesses inconceivable confidence. His speech is immaculate. His voice is pleasing. One never has enough of seeing him. His form is incomparable. He is not stained by the realm of desire. He is not stained by the realm of form. He is not affected by the formless realm. He is completely and utterly liberated from the aggregates. He is not possessed with elements. His senses are controlled. He has completely cut all binds. He is liberated from torment. He is liberated from existence. He has crossed over the river. He is perfected in all the wisdoms. He abides in the wisdom of the blessed ones of the past, present, and future. He does not abide in the extreme of nirvana. He abides in the ultimate perfection. He dwells on the level where he sees all sentient beings. Youth, all these are the perfect virtues of the greatness of the Buddha, the Tathagata.

—CHAPTER 19

Just like the Buddha of our time, if you praise all buddhas and bodhisattvas, chant their names, and make offerings, you too will quickly gain samadhi. You do not have to take my word for it—it becomes clear in personal practice how uttering praises and making offerings fuels your ability to enter the profound dimensions of meditation. Without offering, you will feel stuck, the meditation will be dry, your path will feel forced.

It is said that because Shakyamuni Buddha praised the previous buddhas, it naturally followed that they became his gurus. Just as Shakyamuni Buddha praised and served the buddhas with skill, exalting them with every action, so should we.

> Youthful Moon, it being so, if you desire this samadhi and wish to swiftly, truly realize unsurpassable, perfect, and complete awakening, you too have to endeavor in making offerings, paying homage, and offering service to the tathagatas as I did.
>
> —CHAPTER 2

The sutras and tantras outline the benefits of offering in many ways. All of the different explanations come down to reducing attachment and clinging. As we train in the Dharma, our clinging shifts from worldly objects to "spiritual" objects. We become obsessed with *our* merit, *our* discipline. Through offering, we bring material and spiritual clinging on to the path. When good experiences arise from training, we can also offer those experiences to the buddhas and bodhisattvas.

The Buddha mentions three kinds of offering. The first offering has to do with cleaning the altar, beautifying the temple, and giving flowers and incense. In other words, we express reverence for the practice space. We show and enhance our appreciation through physical actions.

The second kind of offering is actually that of benefiting others. The Buddha said that when we offer service to our fellow beings, it is the same as offering service to the Buddha himself. To sentient beings we offer material objects to protect their bodies, we offer words and physical support to protect them from fear, and we offer the Dharma to bring them to awakening. The Buddha said that a person who always offers the Dharma will maintain the Dharma, and his perception of the world will also become pure.

The third offering is to engage in virtue without attachment. Free from the eight worldly concerns, we practice with mindfulness, gentleness, skill, and kindness. That is offering.

Youth, what does it mean to train in samadhi?

Youth, listen well: With their minds immersed in great compassion, bodhisattva mahasattvas endeavor in making offerings . . . to the tathagatas and those gone beyond. They then dedicate these roots of virtue to the attainment of samadhi. They do not make offerings to the tathagatas with the hope of obtaining anything; they do not hope for

the objects of their desires, or for enjoyments, high
rebirth, or followers, but think only of the Dharma.

—CHAPTER 6

We need to know how to harvest our current wealth in order to transform it into Dharma. If we have resources or wealth and we don't give, it means we have stingy tendencies. Stinginess affects the person who is stingy as much as the person who would otherwise receive the gift. A stingy person fails to use their wealth skillfully, fails to accumulate merit, and does not move any closer to awakening. Such a person also fails to invest in their future rebirth.

If one praises a particular buddha and makes offerings to that buddha with the aspiration to be born in that buddha's pure land or in a heavenly realm, then one begins to assemble the conditions for such a rebirth. Of course, offerings and aspirations must be accompanied by virtuous Dharma practice in order to condition the mind stream to be experienced as a heavenly realm.

If you make unsurpassable offerings
to Maitreya Buddha
and uphold the sublime Dharma,
you will be reborn in Sukhavati.

—CHAPTER 18

If someone has wealth and knows how to give, generosity becomes the force that drives them toward the samadhi that surpasses any type of worldly enjoyment. For example,

I know a person who is very intelligent. She always comes to me with the question, "Rinpoche, when do you plan to do your great accomplishment pujas this year?" These are the intensive practices that take place in our monastery. For nine days, hundreds of monks meditate and do Vajrayana practices, gathering tremendous merit. This woman is always eager to sponsor these pujas. But whenever I say, "I need shoes," she has no interest in buying them. She wants to give money for large events that accumulate great merit. Supporting the serious spiritual practice of monks, nuns, and lay practitioners reaps more virtue than offering material things like clothes and shoes.

We need to know how to give in a way that will also bring about physical benefit for those around us. For example, I have another sponsor who has a lot of money. This sponsor purchased a painting for me worth almost thirty thousand dollars. What am I to do with this? With the same amount of money, they could have fed and supported the practice of so many of the monks and nuns at our monastic institutions.

Another student gave me a small, strange-looking sculpture. It's pink and green and doesn't look like anything in particular—I guess it's art. I'm pretty sure it has some value, but I don't know who would buy it, and I can't sell it. I certainly can't throw it out. So what to do?

I went to another student's house to perform a puja. At the end of the ceremony, they placed three pounds of silver on the table in front of me. I asked them, "What is this for?" They responded, "It's for your mandala offering." Now this was an intelligent act of generosity. They didn't spend money on other things; they knew that I was going to use this silver for merit-accumulation practices. Offerings that can be used to accumulate further merit and offerings that can lead to the direct physical benefit of others are superior to offerings that we personally value but which cannot be utilized. With respect to the Buddha, you can offer anything you value. But when you give to the sangha you should really think about what is useful. The intention behind unusable offerings can be noble, but if noble intention is coupled with functionality, you can aid many people. You should offer so that your mind proceeds along the path of Dharma and in a way that continuously contributes to the outpouring of your wisdom and the wisdom of all beings. You need to know how to extract the essence of accumulation during your practices of generosity.

The sutras enumerate what we can offer. To start with, one can offer clothing, medicine, practical items, and incense. Whatever we are able to use, whatever is important to us, whatever is socially valued, we offer to the enlightened ones. Whatever we gather, the merit we gain, we dedicate to achieving enlightenment. These offerings are the roots that nourish the beautiful tree of samadhi. We also traditionally say that the karmic worldly effect of offering is that we become a little wealthier, we are reborn in a place with more freedoms and resources, and we become less fearful and more confident.

In Shantideva's *Way of the Bodhisattva,* there are many explanations on how to offer—the physical methods and so forth. Learning offering rituals is a process that takes time and instruction from a teacher. But in the beginning, we offer in simple ways. If we come across a flower on the path home, we can place it before an image of the Buddha. If we see a particularly extraordinary sunset, we can think, "I offer this to the buddhas and bodhisattvas so that all beings may awaken to their intrinsic nature." Mental offering reduces regret and attachment, and contributes to the power of our aspirations. Making mental offerings on top of physical offerings is similar to the way in which we endeavor in the bodhichitta of aspiration while carrying out enlightened intent through the bodhichitta of application.

2ND: GIVE WITH THE MIND

To offer on the mental level, we imagine giving the buddhas and bodhisattvas all of the outer offerings: billions of butter lamps, forests and streams, fine vehicles and clothing—all the things we desire. On the inner level, we offer our body and the virtues we have accumulated. On the secret level, we offer the very realization of samadhi. We are always free to offer our Buddha-nature in a single moment to the buddhas and bodhisattvas.

> Youth, since this is the case, offerings are made to the tathagatas without perceiving the tathagatas, without ascertaining the self, and without hoping for karmic fruition.
> —CHAPTER 6

A skilled practitioner actually expects nothing when he makes offerings. He does not cling to a karmic reward. To be free of expectations is called "the mind of the Dharma." Practitioners come to know this mind of the Dharma by offering in a state that is free from characteristics. In this way they come to meet the ultimate buddha, also known as the *dharmakaya buddha*.

As long as subject-object duality exists, we do not meet the dharmakaya buddha, who is free from characteristics. Even if we recall the amazing qualities of the buddhas and bodhisattvas, we are still in the process of thinking. It is impossible to cling to any concept and still meet the dharmakaya buddha. The Buddha therefore says that the proper method of offering is to be free from seeing the Tathagata, the Buddha; to abandon hope for a positive karmic return; and to be without the view that "someone" is making the offering. This is called a "pure, threefold feast."

First, develop the ability to make offerings to the buddhas without wanting anything in return and dedicate the merit to all beings. Then, develop the ability to see the threefold emptiness of the Buddha (the object of offering), the self (the subject who makes the offering), and the action (the offering itself). If we can offer like this, the Buddha says that we will gain authentic enlightenment.

Every time you make an offering, dedicate the merit. Seal the virtue by mentally giving it all away. Dedication becomes a kind of second offering. Think, "Through this merit may all beings reach omniscience. May it defeat the enemy, negative deeds. From the stormy waves of birth, old age, illness, and death, from samsara's ocean, may we all be free." The merit that you dedicate is never lost. It will carry you until you wake up completely.

Becoming a Generous Stream

1. Clean your altar and respectfully make physical offerings to the representations of enlightenment. Traditionally, we offer (1) water for washing; (2) water for drinking; (3) incense; (4) flowers; (5) lights, candles, or butter lamps; (6) perfume; (7) food; and (8) a symbol of music.

2. Throughout your day take every opportunity to benefit others. This includes physical offerings, the offering of protecting others, the offering of the truth of the Dharma, and the offering of engaging in virtue without attachment. Become a stream of generosity, benefiting everyone you meet. Whenever you see someone, think, "How can I help you?"

3. As you walk through the world, make the inner offerings of pure motivation, letting go, and sincere regret for negative actions.

4. Offer through the practice of dedicating your personal virtue. Make aspirations for the enlightenment of all beings.

7

True Discipline

You will be filled with wisdom and bring it to perfection.
You will follow in the footsteps of the Buddha . . .
you will not stray from your commitments . . .
you will achieve nirvana . . .
you will obtain samadhi.

—CHAPTER 28

HOW MANY TIMES did the Buddha give the wisdom of his practice to us? After his enlightenment he did not just sit in the beauty of the forest and watch the leaves fall for the rest of his life. If meditating alone in the forest could save the world, he would have stayed on his cushion of grass. Instead, when the Buddha was urged by Brahma to teach, he accepted to walk in the world and give his liberating instruction to countless beings. To offer people the knowledge of the Dharma is to offer them the chance to obtain an inconceivable fruit. But if we are to offer the Dharma with skill, we first need to attain the results. To this end, we need discipline. Discipline comes from the motivation to offer genuinely, without hypocrisy, the teachings that will lead beings to the radiant fruit of the practice.

When it comes to the Mahayana, the first level of discipline is to physically abstain from harming beings. The second level is to continuously practice the Dharma. The third level of discipline is to bring the results of your practice into the world. The first is easiest—you can run away to a cave and not harm anyone. More challenging is actually training in the view and cultivation of Dharma, but this can also be done on a lonely mountainside. Still more challenging is the actual Dharma activity. Our job is to develop the mindfulness that embraces all three.

1ST: DO NOT HURT ANYONE

Youth, what is this samadhi that fully reveals the equal nature of all things? It is the commitments of body, speech, and mind. It is pure action, beyond any reference point, with full knowledge of the aggregates.

—CHAPTER 1

When the Buddha first turned the Wheel of Dharma, he taught the *listeners* his foundational teachings: to be attentive to their bodily actions, then to their speech, and then to their mental activity. But when he introduced the Great Vehicle through the second phase of his teachings, he focused primarily on paying careful attention to the mind. When your body and speech are under control, your mind becomes stable. Likewise, when your mind is stable, your body and speech are careful.

Carefulness is mindfulness. When we are mindful, we recollect the way things are. To understand this is both simple and deep. When we are mindful, we do not forget impermanence, suffering, selflessness, or emptiness. We act with the pure conduct that arises naturally when the mind never strays from the goal of enlightenment. Within the intention to liberate all beings, we practice the six paramitas. When we wake in the morning, move through our day, drive our car, and drink our coffee, we must never forget the aim to liberate all beings from suffering. This is the way of the Mahayana sutras.

As soon as we lose the mindfulness that recalls the need to liberate all beings, we become hypocrites. So much of the path is about abstaining from hypocrisy, and the root of hypocrisy is insincerity. I used to commit to projects that I suspected I could not complete. Then I would end up disappointing people when I could not fulfill my duties. Now, when I think I cannot do something that is asked of me, I will not say that I can. This is a form of sincerity and is one small way I've been working toward fixing my hypocrisy. Please, look directly at your own hypocritical patterns and fearlessly acknowledge them. We know the ways we are undisciplined; relief comes when we are transparent with others and ourselves.

There are desire hypocrites, aversion hypocrites, and ignorance hypocrites. Desire hypocrites say anything to achieve a calculated result. Aversion hypocrites enact a subtle form of lying to themselves and to others. These aversion hypocrites can feel righteous while standing up against social or structural injustice, yet their language is the language of war, and it doesn't reflect the compassion that might appear to be motivating them to act. The anger of such a person is not "wrathful compassion," though that person may like to believe it is. The action of an anger hypocrite is blinded by fury. As for ignorance hypocrites, they simply don't know what they are doing.

Discipline means recognizing our hypocrisy and knowing that it hurts others, knowing we can dispel it, and knowing how to improve our view and conduct. We need to be convinced of this. "I know I can improve!" is a phrase to which we continuously return. Discipline is not motivated by fear or self-punishment. Discipline comes from the confidence and dignity of realizing we are not static beings with set characters. Our core is wisdom and compassion, and discipline is the way—through skill and carefulness—that we align our actions with our fundamental dignity. We don't need to beat ourselves bloody with a stick. We just have to ask ourselves, "Am I being careful?"

There are also people who have listened to many teachings, have reflected upon them to some degree, and believe that they are therefore practicing the Dharma. They can quote the words of the Buddha and put together beautiful Dharma talks, but they do not guard the actions of their body, speech, and mind. In fact, they will sometimes twist scripture to justify or excuse their harmful activity. The Buddha warns us to guard against falling into this type of trap.

2ND: TRAIN IN THE VIEW, CULTIVATE THE UNDERSTANDING OF DHARMA

If, after you have understood a multitude of teachings,
you have enough of studies and do not guard your
    discipline,
corrupt discipline will bring you to the lower realms,
where all your learning cannot protect you.

—CHAPTER 9

Simply *knowing* how to be disciplined will not save you from the fruit of impulsive action. Discipline means ensuring that our mind does not swing like a monkey from impulse to impulse. If the mind does not involuntarily swing, then the commitments of body and speech are easier to keep. We must do our best to abstain from substances and conditions that cause our mind to be erratic. When the mind is erratic, suffering blooms.

For example, substances such as alcohol are traditionally considered unskillful because they make it easier for the mind to swing. Let me be clear: alcohol in and of itself is not bad, but a swinging mind is harmful. Sometimes alcohol is medicine. The same can be said of other substances. People suffering from multiple sclerosis sometimes take marijuana as medicine, and pain pills are used to ease the intense physical suffering of hospital patients. Extremely advanced Vajrayana practitioners might eat the hallucinogenic seed of a certain flower just once to see how malleable the mind is, to see that everything is like an illusion.

Substances are just substances, but they produce harm when we ingest them with the intention of wading further into delusion. Discipline means abstaining from the conditions that thrust us deeper into delusion.

We are also taught to guard our body, speech, and mind against the influence of unwholesome companions. We do not judge people who are unruly or negative, but we are advised to protect the mind from swinging, which naturally happens when we continuously associate with such companions. On the flip side, the tradition offers us a beautiful metaphor about associating with virtuous people. It is said that if you place a normal piece of wood in a sandalwood forest, in time that normal piece of wood will begin to take on the sweet smell of sandalwood. In the same way, even if we are a normal person, if we associate with noble companions, we will naturally begin to give rise to the qualities of virtue and wisdom.

Nowadays Buddhist discipline is often misinterpreted. People think Buddhism is *against* this and that, which is really not how we think about discipline at all. Buddhism advises us to keep the commitments that will contribute to our awakening. The Buddhist teachings say that eating too much food is harmful, but Buddhism never says anything negative about food itself. We acknowledge that a stuffed belly makes the mind dull. This is also the case with sleeping excessively or not resting enough. Discipline is about creating the conditions for a healthy, stable mind. If we are intent on awakening to supreme bliss, we must be aware of and abstain from the conditions and activities that disrupt the mind. It is very logical.

In the beginning, meditation practice is heavily influenced by the people who surround us, the substances we take, even the clothes we wear. If we want to generate genuine samadhi, then we must persevere in intelligently working with these factors. As a rule, remember this: when your mind swings, you are in for more suffering. When your mind does not swing, you automatically know it does not swing. This is stability.

The scriptures that outline the conduct of monks say that monks should not handle gold. But if a monk is completely free from all attachment, and someone hands him a suitcase with a million dollars' worth of gold inside, he can take it. In the Mahayana, we verify our conduct by the quality of our minds, not by scripture alone. Aversion, attachment, and ignorance must be abandoned. If there is consistent mindfulness, then there is discipline. As we begin to stabilize the commitments of our physical conduct, on a deeper level we also begin to stabilize the mindfulness that recollects the emptiness of the five aggregates, which make up the entirety of our experiences. Stability in this recognition ensures that we do not break our vows.

> Whoever knows the five aggregates to be empty
> understands them to be naturally empty and selfless.
> Any physical action becomes pure conduct
> and their vows are never broken.
>
> —CHAPTER 39

A bodhisattva said to the Buddha, "Whenever I practice Dharma, I experience obstacles. Why is this?" The Buddha said, "Of course this is the case. When you practice, you will have obstacles. If you don't practice, you don't need obstacles. You are the obstacle." For me, this is one of the best things to hear. If you practice, the demon Mara is going to get in the way. When I say "Mara" I do not mean some ghost out there waiting to get you. Mara really refers to negative emotions. You will see Mara clearly when you turn the tide against your own habits. Mara becomes significantly pronounced in the case of the practitioner. If you are not practicing, you are too close to detect Mara; you are Mara.

Nonetheless, human beings are constantly externalizing the demon Mara, who at root is ego-clinging. They feel like there is something *out there* waiting to harm them. In the Vajrayana, we employ many methods of practice to reduce this fear, such as visualizing an indestructible barrier around our practice place. But honestly, the best way to reduce our fear is to practice emptiness. So we employ these methods until we have manifested the ability to genuinely practice emptiness. As soon as we can practice emptiness, the discipline of maintaining the correct view is our armor against Mara.

What is emptiness? It is not easy to describe. The Buddha used many words to point toward it. He said it is unborn, unceasing, inexpressible, and free from characteristics—it has always been like this. He said it is naturally pure and that the bodhisattva who sees this knows the truth.

The Mahayana teaches that, from the beginning, everything is peace. This is what we will come to understand. It is not correct to hear about emptiness, intellectually conclude that phenomena don't truly exist, and then leave it at that. This ultimately will not benefit you. If you hold this assumption and I slap you very hard, you're instantly going to believe that phenomena exist. The genuine acceptance of emptiness is to see that phenomena actually, by nature, do not have substantial existence. They were never truly born and therefore never cease. Nobody made them that way—I certainly didn't do it, and you didn't do it. All phenomena are just naturally like that.

> Acceptance of the selfless nature of phenomena
> means perceiving selflessness without afflictive
>   emotions
> and knowing all phenomena to be like the sky:
> those are the reasons for calling it acceptance.
> —CHAPTER 4

We realize this through assembling the conditions for proper practice, engaging in generosity, keeping our discipline, clarifying our view, and training in meditation. If we want to actually see this, we need to uphold all of the elements of the path. The alternative is mere wishful thinking. If, however, we are able to give rise to the realization of emptiness, we can become totally and completely free.

A bodhisattva who has this wisdom no longer has attachment to the objects of the sense consciousnesses because he knows that those objects are insubstantial. Neither will he experience aversion, nor operate under the heavy veils of ignorance. If he sees there is nothing to be desired, how will he desire? He is free from the objects of Mara, and he maintains the pure world of the Buddha. He ripens himself through the wisdom of this realization.

Although this realization of emptiness is actually beyond expression, we nonetheless approach it through the discipline of recollection. The supreme way to keep discipline is to recall that phenomena are essentially peace from the beginning and to see the three realms as a dream. The traditional examples are that all phenomena are like illusions, hallucinations, an echo, a visual defect, a magic show, a reflection in water, or space.

What does it mean that all phenomena are like dreams? A dream is a result of conditions that occur in waking life, and when we fall asleep we see the imprint of those conditions and take the dream to be real. Even if we know we are dreaming, only fifty percent of the problem has been solved. We may recognize that we are dreaming but we still dream, so how do we wake from that? Similarly, in our waking life, we may come to see that we are within the illusion of samsara. We can understand that the flowers on the roadside and the dirty pockets on the back of airplane seats are illusions, but still we do not wake up. We take up the Buddhist path with discipline in order to rouse ourselves from the dream of samsara. We are not yet out. This is our project; it is why we practice. If we do not have discipline, it is going to be impossible for us to wake up.

Similarly, appearances are like hallucinations because

we perceive things that are not there. We may determine a set of conditions to be good and feel that they are permanent, but that is a wrong view.

Things are like an echo because we are in the flux of illusory sound and judgment. We grasp, we name, we say, "I like this," and "I don't like that." When people praise us, we love it. Yet each moment of praise comes and disappears like a finger snap. Each word comes and goes right away—why do we hold on to them? If we hold praise, it is like holding an echo. There is nothing there to grasp on to. Who is making the echo? We are. We run praise through our minds again and again, making a noise that cannot last, attached to a sound that does not stay. A person praises you once, and you praise yourself a hundred times.

Appearances are like a visual defect. Sometimes I will look at someone and think, "That guy hates me." In actuality he is having problems with his marriage, and the anger I see has nothing to do with me. I create an entire story out of a look on his face. "This man despises me because I know my friend told him that I didn't like his attitude." On and on I go about all this stuff that is completely unrelated.

We say that all phenomena are like a reflection because everything that you see displayed upon the surface of the world is mind. We don't see the actual substance of mind in the external world, but when our disposition changes we see the external world change. The substance of a mind does not "go out" somewhere, but we see our mental disposition manifesting as physical appearance.

The example of a magic show is a good analogy for our

fantasizing. We create, we daydream, we think of fantastic worlds. Without effort we spin stories in which we are the hero or villain, and these stories arise before us magically— unreal, yet entangling us still.

The analogy of space simply refers to the unimpeded, empty expanse in which all things inseparably arise.

3RD: WALK WITH REALIZATION

Since they cannot truly perceive or apprehend these phenomena, it is said that they have no attachment, anger, ignorance, or wrong view, and they are in meditative equipoise.

They are said to be free of conceptual elaborations . . . to have gone into bliss and attained fearlessness. They have discipline, wisdom, knowledge, merit, miraculous powers, mindfulness, intelligence, realization, and conscientiousness. . . . They have no afflictive emotions. . . .

They are foe-destroyers. . . . Their minds are liberated by true knowledge.

Their wisdom is liberated. . . . They are called brahmins . . . monks . . . supreme beings.

—CHAPTER 9

The great Indian yogi Naropa cast off his monastic attire and said, "Previously I was ordained as a monk, but now I am a true monk." His meaning is expressed in the *King of Meditation Sutra*: a real monk, a real Brahmin, an authentic holy person, is one who is always free from the three poisons. People sometimes criticize the Vajrayana masters who are married but maintain the Dharma robes. If you look, however, they are displaying the intent first set forth in the Mahayana sutras.

When you maintain the view of dreamlike appearances and the view of selflessness, you are free from "I." When you are free from "I," you are free from fear and the possibility of being terrorized by negative emotions. Free from terror, you are unmoving. Unmoving, obstacles cannot affect you. A bodhisattva who is unaffected in this way can fearlessly benefit others. The Buddha said that if you maintain this type of pure discipline, you can enter a den of thieves, of liars, of creators of negative karma, even a nest of snakes, and you will remain untouched. This is always mentioned in the sutras. People ask what the benefit of "no I" is. There is the answer.

If you keep discipline, people will praise you. This naturally happens. But if you are an aspiring bodhisattva and you revel in praise, then you are not really upholding the practice. Similarly, if everyone is criticizing you and you feed the anger that arises, you are not in line with the teachings. In order to keep totally and completely pure discipline, you must become like the sky.

> Just as the sky is immaculate,
> utterly pure, and naturally luminous,
> likewise, pure vows of the body
> can never be verbally expressed.
> —CHAPTER 39

We cannot truly speak of the pure conduct of a bodhi-sattva's body; it arises out of their realization of emptiness. Natural, empty luminosity is the transcendent characteristic of appearances and it cannot be articulated. When we go beyond our fixation on the gross body into immaculate, sky-like space, our body holds the ultimate vow. This is also impossible to speak of. Whoever truly sees this cannot abandon the discipline of the body.

Maintaining Discipline

- Be mindful of your actions and careful in all moments of daily life. Evaluate yourself: Am I hurting anyone?

- In your formal meditation sessions, alternate between generating compassion for all beings and recalling that everything is an illusion.

- Remember that emptiness is the nature of your body, thoughts, feelings, and everything that appears. This empty nature was never created and will never decline or decrease. It is always pure and free. Recalling this and maintaining this is the beginning of true discipline.

PATIENT AND UNHARMED

1ST: FUEL NO AGGRESSION

In this world people follow many creeds.
Holding anger toward none,
and meeting them with compassion:
these are the qualities of the first level
of patience.

—CHAPTER 7

THERE IS A green and verdant mountain in China where monastics train in the practices of Amitabha Buddha, the buddha of infinite light. They chant his mantra with great devotion, they pray, and they meditate on the scriptures that describe his pure land. I heard recently that a bird flew to this place, landed next to one of the monks, and chirped "Amitabha." Imagine, day and night you train in the practice of Amitabha, and out of the blue an ordinary sparrow perches next to you and says, "Amitabha." Needless to say, the monks took this as an auspicious sign. It gave them confidence that they were practicing correctly.

Most of us do not train under such circumstances. We

have nightmares, live in dirty cities, people curse at us, the surroundings seem to be contradicting our efforts to practice. The bird outside our window is definitely not chirping "Amitabha." In these circumstances, how are we to verify that our practice is going well? We need to take an honest look at the motivation we bring to our practice. If our motivation is pure, in that it is endowed with compassion and, to the best of our ability, free from clinging to self and other, then we are training well. The truth is, until we attain buddhahood we can always give rise to more pure experiences. Because we have never experienced a completely pure motivation, we do not know what it is actually like; so we need to rely on something that can contextualize our current level of practice and show us where we must go. I was fortunate enough to have reliable teachers, so I depended on them to help me develop my motivation.

Many of us do not have continuous access to a reliable teacher, and so we depend on the reliable instructions of the Buddha that come from the sutras. We must see for ourselves, in a very sharp way, whether our aspirations align with the Buddha's teachings. We must read the biographies of great masters and understand the vigor with which they practiced, the vastness of their patience, and the purity of their motivation.

Our view, meditation, and conduct should always be the same—our conduct has to be an expression of our motivation. For most of us, this isn't always the case. We may sit in meditation and examine the constituents of our bodies, reminding ourselves, "No eye, no ear, no nose, no tongue, no body, and no mind," just as it is said in the *Heart Sutra*. We may penetrate deep into these matters, giving rise to an experience of space. But do we then carry this spaciousness off the cushion and into our relationships? Do we practice the patience of being free from anger, of being compassionate? Do we hold this view when we encounter people who believe differently than we do? We may meditate on emptiness but still desire to attain enlightenment only for ourselves. In this case our motivation, view, meditation, and conduct are not aligned. Samadhi is naturally present when we bring these into alignment.

We usually have at least one companion who is always asking us to verify the legitimacy of our practice. This person tries to tear holes in our philosophical positions, or if they are challenging us on religious grounds, they will make demands such as, "Show me a miracle of the Buddha!" Our response should always be calm, interested, and offering an appropriate explanation for our view. Keeping quiet is not the right way. We should explain with patience, without being driven by our afflictions, and with correct understanding. In this way, the people who challenge us help us refine our practice and reveal gaps in our knowledge. They help us develop patience, and they help us train in compassion.

Compassion and patience are closely related. It is not that we walk through the world thinking, "I really am superior to everyone. I know more and am endowed with wisdom, and because of this I have compassion." This is totally incorrect. Compassion involves the respect for intrinsic equality. Compassion in Buddhism means recognizing that we are all on precisely the same level—we all just want to be happy. We have to exert the patience to calibrate mentally toward this recognition. A natural patience arises when we begin to experience the intrinsic sameness of all beings.

We must always notice how we approach other people. So, again, vigorous practitioners often get deluded into thinking that they are superior to other people. We need to train in thinking that we are either equal to a person or lower than that person. In fact, we should understand anyone who offers us even a single word of Dharma to be a teacher. This is how we can begin to reduce our pride.

> They must perceive all the buddhas and bodhisattvas as their teachers. With joy and respect, they must also perceive whoever delivers them these Dharma discourses as their teachers.
>
> —CHAPTER 18

At the same time, we engage in the meditation of exchanging self with other. Further, whenever we talk about meditation practice with another practitioner, we should speak from a place that acknowledges that the person before us is a *better* meditator! If we think, "I am great, I am good!" or feel that we have entered into some safety zone of virtue, we actually misunderstand the tenuousness and impermanence of our current situation. We need to become comfortable with recognizing the equality of everyone in the light of impermanence.

The knowledge that all phenomena are illusory
is beyond the scope of reasoning—
it does not falter from the ground of increasing
   wisdom.
These are the qualities of the first level of patience.
                                        —CHAPTER 7

On the highest level, we can remember that the ground of everything is the pervasiveness of wisdom. This is the recollection of our intrinsic nature. The ground is pure and illusory, the path is pure and illusory, and the result is the realization of complete purity. Whether we practice calm-abiding or profound emptiness, we must continuously recall the complete purity of everything. This pure ground is the basis for supreme patience.

The Buddha gives us a method for attaining the freedom of patience. We have a choice to make. Are we truly going to apply the method and integrate it into our experience? Or are we going to manipulate the method according to our current habits and desires? To genuinely apply the method, free from manipulation, is patience. By training in seeing all phenomena to be sky-like, we approach selflessness, which has no afflictions and leads us into emptiness.

In the Mahayana sutras we are taught to train in a spacious type of meditation, in which the "object" of meditation is actually ungraspable, limitless. Emerging from that state, we enter the post-meditation state and go about our lives. In the post-meditation state, we continue to see everything as illusion. In this illusory view, attachment is not strong, and thus wisdom increases. This is the beginning of patience.

The Tibetan word *ngejung* is usually translated as renunciation, but it has yet another meaning—something akin to "the wish to achieve." The positive aspect of renunciation corresponds to the patience required to achieve this view of sky-like phenomena. When this view is attained, phenomena have no characteristics, and we are free from attachment and suffering.

Simply practice. Drop your anger when it arises. This is part of the first level of patience. Be peaceful, commit virtuous deeds, and take the goodness of the teachings into your heart. Don't have anger toward non-Buddhist views. Undercut your pride. If someone publicly scolds you, take that moment as an opportunity to watch your reactivity. The concept of Buddha should not be solely affixed to a single historic individual; instead, see all experience as the spontaneous teaching of Buddha. Despite the constant changing of the four elements, you must remain one-pointedly set upon the goal of buddhahood. All of this is the practice of the first level of patience.

> Whichever excellent teaching you hear,
> being free of doubt regarding the Buddha's speech
> and confident in the Dharma of all the victorious
>   ones—
> these are the qualities of the first type of patience.
> —CHAPTER 7

If we don't listen to the teachings, then we won't be able to practice. All of it—our conduct, our ability to train in meditation, our insight—begins with listening. Therefore, we practice the patience of listening and the patience of reflection, which dispels doubts.

The sutra mentions that we must have confidence in the victorious ones, the buddhas and bodhisattvas. In order to do that, we have to investigate their qualities and the teachings they espouse. What philosophical systems and schools do the noble ones ascribe to?

In actuality, the Buddha does not subscribe to any school. It is impossible for the Awakened One to be bound by the limitations of a conceptual system. The Buddha is one who has gone beyond the afflictive and cognitive obscurations and attained victory. What, then, can the Buddha teach? The true Buddha can only teach what is useful for bringing beings to liberation. He teaches only that which will escort beings beyond affliction—precisely in accordance with their unique karma and capacity. The awakened ones teach that which brought them to realization.

> The Dharma that you have trained in
> is the exact Dharma that you teach.
> —CHAPTER 13

Sometimes we get into this funny way of thinking in which we imagine the Buddha to be Buddhist. We wonder, who does the Buddha take refuge in? Does he understand the four noble truths? If he *understands* them, doesn't that mean he has a mind? If so, that means he has the source of affliction and is a sentient being, not a Buddha. We need to think deeply about these types of questions. The key is always to return to the title of "Victorious One" and think about what that really means. Does it refer to victory over physical enemies? No. It refers to having victory over doubt, victory over afflictions, victory over incorrect views, and ultimately, victory over all concepts. When we take the time to thoroughly investigate, we practice the first level of patience.

2ND: MEDITATE

Resting in meditation as they stand and speak,
resting in meditation as they sit and walk,
the wise bring samadhi to perfection.
These are the qualities of the second level of patience.

—CHAPTER 7

Meditation needs to become continuous. Although we speak of meditation in terms of formal sessions and the post-meditation state, we ultimately will go beyond the division of these two. Continuous practice opens into samadhi. We need to be vast in our understanding and application. Continuous meditation is the second level of patience.

Through the power of *shamatha*, agitation vanishes.
Through *vipashyana*, you become like a mountain.

All beings together could not disturb you.
This is taught to be the second level of patience.
—CHAPTER 7

In the meditation section of this book, we will learn how the Buddha taught meditation in the root text of the *King of Meditation Sutra*. For now, know this: *shamatha*, or calm-abiding practice, keeps your mind from swinging. Through it you become more stable. Within this stability, the weaknesses of individual sentient beings become clearer to you. Attainment of shamatha grants the ability to bring these sentient beings onto the path. This is an aspect of the second type of patience. *Vipashyana*, special insight practice, develops steadiness. Through vipashyana, the mind is no longer a "thing" to be influenced—which is actually a very profound understanding.

Through training in meditation our "gut feeling" improves. We notice that our intuition is dramatically enhanced, and this is the first taste of how an accomplished meditator can be breathtakingly precise. If you practice to the point at which your hope has almost vanished and all expectation ceased, whomever you look at will be so much more transparent. The noisiness of distraction is gone. You know exactly what to say to make someone happy or cure what ails them. Your activity may actually be inscrutable to the person in front of you, or it may seem to be contrary to conventional interpretations of compassion, but it is actually very powerful and kind. This is the benefit of samadhi. You know how to teach the Dharma in accordance with the person who is receiving the teaching. You are not going to offer words beyond that person's comprehension, nor are you going to give them less than they need at that moment. All of this is associated with training in and stabilizing the second level of patience. When you attain this clarity and insight, you create the conditions for a mountain-like mind.

3RD: REMAIN UNHARMED

Not gladdened by acquisition,
nor saddened by deprivation,
but always with a mountain-like mind—
these are the qualities of the third level of patience.

—CHAPTER 7

Whenever I stress about money, wealth doesn't seem to come. Whenever I don't worry too much about accumulating wealth, resources seem to flow in more naturally. People who really take karma to heart sometimes hope that virtuous practice will bring wealth, and this sneaks its way deep into their motivation. If wealth doesn't come rolling in, they get anxious and irritated and upset. As lay practitioners, we of course need some safety net. We have families and we must live—but beyond that, if you don't ruminate too much and are a genuine practitioner, wealth will sometimes start coming from unexpected directions.

Whatever comes, we shouldn't be too excited. Whatever goes, we shouldn't be too depressed. How you react to the coming and going of resources is a very fine reflection of the stability of your mind. When you have a comfortable life, practice may actually not go so well. You get a little lazy. But suddenly, some health issue arises, or a family problem, and you begin to practice very intently. When you feel very comfortable, you can devalue the spiritual path. Buddhism is not against comfort, but it is against the delusion that anything other than Dharma can create lasting satisfaction. Buddhism always reminds us: "Impermanence, impermanence!"

Impermanence shakes us out of delusion. If you are neither overjoyed when you accumulate wealth nor depressed about losing some money, it means that wealth is not excessively affecting your mind. This shows that your mind is steady, and a steady mind both practices well and is the result of good practice.

> The experience of the buddhas as well as their
>   methods
> and the conduct of these buddhas—
> all are practiced by bodhisattvas.
> These are the qualities of the third level of patience.
> —CHAPTER 7

The Buddha displayed ultimate sincerity. For that reason, we should read the life story of the Buddha as well as the *Jataka Tales*, which detail his previous lives, so that we too can understand how to be sincere practitioners. The Buddha can emotionally influence us through the narrative of his story. Stories can teach us in a way that philosophy cannot. Philosophy doesn't create an intimate relationship with the body of the Buddha, which walked in the world as a radiant sun of love and wisdom. When we read the biographies of great masters and practitioners, we can start to see the same way that the Buddha sees—without judgment, with purity and equality, with the loving-kindness that holds each and every being as dearer to him than his own body. When we read about the actions of the noble ones, we cannot help but carry those actions into our own lives. A bodhisattva replicates the activities of the Buddha in their own life, as best they can.

There is a practice called *Abandon and Purify*. In this practice, all that one possesses is given to others. The practitioner literally gives away everything they own aside from the clothes on their back. We make a connection to these practices first by marveling at others who do them and rejoicing in that. Then, if it is skillful and if we have the courage, we can eventually carry them out ourselves. Through such practices of patience, one gains access to the realization that goes beyond birth and death, the realization that all phenomena abide in the *dharmata*, the essence of reality.

> The day a perfect bodhisattva attains
> these three unsurpassable types of patience
> he no longer perceives birth or death
> but all phenomena as abiding in dharmata.
> Thus he ascertains the lack of true establishment:

phenomena are illusory and empty by nature;
emptiness itself cannot be perceived, and there is
no death;
all phenomena are empty by their very essence.

—CHAPTER 7

It is said that if you have transcendent patience, you will not be harmed by fire or water, nor will weapons and poison affect you. Patience gives you a beautiful countenance and an attractive form. Patience reduces the possibility that you will descend to the lower realms of existence, because patience reduces the anger. Conversely, patience is a cause for rebirth in the higher realms as it is both a noble quality and a source from which further noble qualities arise. If you have genuine patience, your body and mind will experience bliss throughout day and night. All of these benefits are mentioned in the *King of Meditation Sutra*.

In sum, the courageous ones endowed with patience see all phenomena to be like an illusion, naturally empty. They see that the essence of everything is empty but do not grasp to it as an object called emptiness. It is not a thing. The essence of emptiness is also empty. Reflect on this. The bodhisattvas no longer see characteristics. Without seeing characteristics, they seize the stronghold of the essence and go beyond birth and death. They acquire the emanation body and can emanate into uncountable worlds in order to benefit the beings of those worlds. This is the fruit of patience.

Clarifying Patience

1. Reflect upon your motivation. In this moment, do you truly have the wish to help others?

2. Do you really understand the correct view? For example, when receiving teachings on selflessness, are you confident in your conceptual understanding? If not, study, reflect, and resolve. If you are confident in your conceptual understanding, practice meditation to experientially relate to that understanding. *View* is engaging the truth. *Meditation* is expanding that truth. *Conduct* is expressing the truth.

3. Ask yourself again and again: How aligned are my view, meditation, and conduct?

4. Be sincere. Ask yourself:

   • Am I humble?

   • Do I see others as equal to myself?

   • Do I possess the sincerity to be a clear witness to my own behavior?

9
JOYFUL EFFORT

1ST: INSPIRE YOURSELF

If, without laziness but with joyful effort,
you truly work toward supreme awakening,
your quest for samadhi is pure.
Therefore, Youth, a bodhisattva
who wishes to cultivate this samadhi
with joyful effort and no regard for
his own life
is always following my example.
—CHAPTER 17

MILAREPA, Tibet's great yogi, lived in snowy caves on wind-swept mountains, wearing only a thin cotton cloth and keeping warm through the power of his yogic ability. He ate only green nettles and was nourished primarily by the food of samadhi. For decades Milarepa stayed alone, diligently training in the pith instructions given to him by his guru, Marpa, and in time he gained perfect awakening.

Another Tibetan master vowed to sit in one spot until he gained realization, just like the Buddha vowed to remain unmoving beneath the Bodhi tree. After a few days, the master became hungry and weak. Four more days passed, and he was on the verge of death—when suddenly, in a moment of clarity, all fear melted away and the light of realization dawned within.

Yet another yogi vowed he would not travel to any town or village to acquire food while practicing beside a small, high-altitude lake. He stayed there through the winter and was snowed in for six months. He had to forage in the cold to stay alive. Sometimes he ate the meat of frozen animals he found, sometimes he was able to pull tubers from the ground, and sometimes he ate dry tufts of grass.

These yogis practiced in austerities in order to stabilize their commitment to realization. Their practices were not undertaken blindly, or with some sort of hazy understanding. In these situations, the masters knew exactly what they were doing. They knew the teachings inside and out. They understood the path and how to traverse it, and then they walked it without doubt. These yogis did not pretend they were more advanced than they actually were; they simply had the ability to train under challenging conditions. They knew what they needed to do, and they lived in the world according to this understanding without any regard for their own lives.

When we speak of the trials of superior yogis, we do not refer simply to discomfort in their knees or pain in the lower back—sometimes their very lives were at stake. Consider the powerful conviction necessary to drive someone to this level of physical commitment. We should all read the life stories of great meditators like Milarepa, because these stories show us what genuine diligence looks like.

We take up meditation practice on the basis of understanding the preciousness of our human life, the impermanent nature of phenomena, the unfailing law of cause and effect, and the defects of remaining within samsara. In order to inspire ourselves, we can remember that the fruits of practice are sublime beyond anything we can imagine. As the Buddha said in a collection of his foundational teachings known as the *Dhammapada*, "Would not a wise man trade a lesser happiness for a greater?"

In this light, we sometimes translate the Tibetan word for diligence as "joyful effort." This is an inspiring way to approach the path. In the beginning, "joyful effort" sounds good, but in reality, exertion is necessary. Eventually you need to be able to sit for many hours. It may sound harsh, but when you sit for three hours, the joyful effort goes away after one hour. Once you have a little stability, you can sit and meditate and have the experience of being very happy. But when you begin to extend the length of time that you sit, you will eventually start to think, "Okay, this is enough. It would be good to do something else. Maybe I should have a snack." When this thought comes, turn your mind to impermanence. Very deliberately think to yourself, "I'm going to die today. I'm going to die right now! I must train!" You need that courageous element of diligence. So, again, while it is good to begin with the pleasant expression "joyful effort," it is good to continue with "diligence" as it is more commonly understood. Then profound insight begins to unfold and true joy pervades.

The *King of Meditation Sutra* says that if your aim is to stabilize samadhi, you must come to a point in training in which you no longer express laziness. If this thought is daunting, it is because you still desire mundane pleasure and mundane success. If you train correctly and pursue samadhi purely, you will find that the path becomes utter joy. Advanced diligence is rooted in this joy. Until that time comes, we persevere.

As was said, the bodhisattva literally chases realization without any thought of preserving their own life. The first step, however, is to understand the path. Without understanding the path, one-pointed exertion in practice is useless. So the bodhisattva understands how to give rise to samadhi, which is precisely what we are clarifying here in this book. We must decisively integrate the instructions we receive into our meditation practice.

Too often our appetite for practice is influenced by the experiences we are having in our meditation practice. If we are having good experiences in meditation, we want to meditate more. But if we have more troublesome circumstances, we are often deterred. The moment of deterrence is an opportunity to see the quality of our diligence. Of course, there is the extreme of being *too* comfortable, the result of which is that we don't feel much need to practice at all.

Unlike a normal person, the diligence of a bodhisattva mahasattva is limited only by the physical conditions that prevent their survival, not by the pain they experience. For this reason, the diligence of bodhisattvas is truly extraordinary.

Little snakes in our retreat place, small bees hovering around our hair in the garden as we meditate, the sounds of cars or people arguing—these are things we eventually stop caring about. When we are no longer flustered, we get excellent results. We will have the experience of being embraced by the buddhas, and our sense of health and fortune will expand.

> You will be embraced by the buddhas and all the
>   gods.
> You will not forget the teachings you have received,
> and you will receive teachings you have not yet heard.
> You will attain the various samadhis, and you will
>   have fewer illnesses.
>
> —CHAPTER 29

When you are diligent, your loved ones become more loving toward you. When you are lazy, most people will not like you, honestly speaking. When you work hard, even if you don't earn much money, but you are exerting yourself in something noble, everyone naturally praises you. If you just sit around and do nothing but eat, your loved ones are going to be annoyed, no matter how old you are. It's very sensible.

In the Dharma it is not so different. If you train with

diligence, you will have the feeling that you are embraced by the buddhas. Knowing you are embraced by the buddhas, you will gain their blessings and qualities. Furthermore, devas are going to protect you and the Dharma protectors are going to keep you afloat. You will understand Dharma and your knowledge will not degenerate. You will encounter teachings you have not heard before, and you will reap the fruits of those new teachings. Even your current practices will produce new realizations. For example, you may currently practice cultivating a little compassion, but when you become admirably diligent, the practice will reach profound depths. You will naturally see with a clarity and compassion that you did not previously have.

Although study and reflection form the bedrock for practice, you will gain more from meditation than from excessively reading Dharma books. Sometimes we read about practices that are too far out of reach. A book can reach you with its words, but you cannot reach the book, so to speak. There is a big difference between reading about the experiences of authentic practitioners and actually sitting down on the cushion to tame your own mind. You must persist and train and gain insight within yourself. This is far more important than reading a book while lying down in your bed and fantasizing about being a great meditator. Throw off this habit of "great meditator" fantasizing and exert yourself in practice.

With diligence, you will master the different meditative states, and you will fall prey to fewer illnesses. Perhaps you will value the circumstances that lead to proper training.

You will eat well and practice well and look after yourself, because, well, you are diligent! When you ask unhealthy people why they don't want to exercise, they sometimes give the honest answer, "I'm lazy." They don't have the diligence to do what must be done to improve their health. When you are practicing well and eating well, you will look like a flower—very clear and shining, full of charisma. This is the benefit of diligence.

The *King of Meditation Sutra* tells us of these benefits. I am not making them up. A sutra will often provide a description of the worldly advantages of practice along with the Dharmic fruition. We can be inspired by the idea that we will become radiant in appearance, and we should. Along with that worldly inspiration, however, we orient ourselves toward the ultimate. We let inspiration be inspiration, and we turn toward the unsurpassable joy of the genuine samadhi. We obtain this joy by exerting ourselves in three areas.

2ND: PURSUE THE RESULT

Bodhisattvas should apply effort in three areas. What are
   these three?
They are the exhaustion of afflictive emotions, becoming
   a field of merit,
and generating roots of virtue with the wish to obtain
   the wisdom of the buddhas—
but not for the sake of experiencing mundane happiness.

—CHAPTER 38

Whatever practice you do, you do it for three primary reasons: (1) to conquer the negative thoughts and emotions, (2) to become a field of merit for yourself and others, and (3) to gain the Buddha's wisdom. Regarding the first of these, you know you are improving on the path when you gain the ability to see how you react, how emotionally uncontrolled you are, how much your thoughts produce further thoughts, and how much attachment you have. It is an excellent sign when you begin to notice these. These afflictions will begin to subside through the power of awareness. Through training correctly, they will exhaust themselves completely.

Khandro Yeshe Tsogyal, the Tibetan consort of Padmasambhava, made a vast aspiration in front of the guru. She said, "May I become like a wish-fulfilling jewel for whoever meets me." This is what the Buddha means when he says we should strive to be a field of merit. You must become a great being—a being with such enormous merit that if someone even thinks of you, even for a single moment, their mind stream is imprinted with your merit. In other words, the force of your wisdom and virtue is so powerful that you benefit beings by simply being on the planet. So, second, you must become a light for the world in that way. If you are a true practitioner, you automatically become a vessel of merit.

Third, whatever practice you do, you must aim for the attainment of wisdom, nothing less. When you focus intently upon the true fruit, you do not take subsidiary paths. You will not waste anything. If you are efficient in your intention, results come quickly.

Look at these three objectives: taming negative thoughts, becoming a field of merit, and gaining wisdom. The first aims to reduce harm, the second to achieve spiritual accomplishment, and the third to increase realization and benefit. One of the ways to say "Buddha" in Tibetan is *chom den dey*. Here, *chom* means "to vanquish," *den* means "to be endowed," and *dey* means "to transcend." The first syllable therefore refers to conquering the negative emotions, the second refers to being endowed with merit and qualities, and the third refers to transcendent wisdom. So, one of the words for "Buddha" is actually composed of the three areas in which you apply effort—the three areas that constitute diligence.

One of Padmasambhava's aspirations was to bring temporary benefit and ultimate bliss to whoever creates a connection with him, regardless of whether that connection is positive or negative. We should also make such aspirations. When we become a genuine field of merit, even the man who ripped us off at the car lot ten years ago will be benefited through his connection to us. This is the impartial compassion that arises from the ocean of merit of a supreme practitioner. The Buddha said that the virtue of a hundred normal people could not compare with the merit of a single authentic practitioner.

To go beyond, *dey*, means to embody wisdom. From the bottom of your heart you must yearn to be inseparable from the great samadhi of wisdom. Exert yourself in yearning for this wisdom.

3RD: REJOICE IN YOUR OWN PRACTICE

When you see diligence in yourself, rejoice. For some time, the path will oscillate between strenuousness and joyful momentum. For example, when writing this book, I went through the *King of Meditation* root text and selected quotes that would be useful to explain, that would help you. This took a lot of exertion, yet there was virtue in it. In the evening, I would close the sutra and lie down, knowing I had engaged in positive activity. I would supplicate the gurus and buddhas and then go to sleep. When I woke up in the morning, I would do some practice, look at the sutra again, mark more quotations, and at night I would sleep again, knowing I had been active for others' sake. With this effort came joy.

I would also like to speak about a particular type of effort that must be exerted in our current times. When you wake up in the morning, please stop yourself from immediately looking at your cell phone. The first thing you should do is practice; set your mind on the Buddha and generate the wish to gather merit and wisdom unceasingly throughout the day. If you open your cell phone right when you wake up, your mind immediately starts racing. Then when you go to practice your mind will not calm down. Sometimes there are things that are very pressing, but even when I am in a time crunch, I delay responding until my morning practice is complete. This is a form of diligence.

If you are diligent, you will gain the qualities of the buddhas. Great beings will come to help you. Like a lotus flower, you will remain untouched by the difficulties and afflictions that cling to suffering beings in the world. Since you are always practicing, your mind is set upon awakening, and obstacles slide off like water. Virtue increases, day and night. If you generate the mind of awakening throughout your day, this will carry over into the dream state. In the dream state you will gather virtue due to this momentum, and your dreams will be saturated with loving-kindness. Imagine what this will be like.

Refining Diligence

1. **Continuously recall impermanence**: Think of your own death and the death of those you hold dear. Remember the preciousness of this very moment, and how rare it is to have the conditions to genuinely practice.

2. **Tame the negative emotions:** See your own afflictions without becoming obsessed with eradicating them. Calmly and continuously practice in order to reduce the power of these afflictions.

3. **Become a field of merit:** Gather merit by doing activities, big and small, that benefit others. The more spacious and profound your motivation, the greater the accumulation. Your motivation should acknowledge the inseparability of all phenomena.

4. **Attain wisdom:** The real samadhi is the empty nature of your mind, which is always present. Recall that all of

the buddhas are not separate from the empty nature, and therefore they are not separate from you. When you continuously remind yourself of this, samadhi increases until realization.

10

VICTORIOUS MEDITATION

Virtuous behavior always comes first,

then skill in casting away conceptions,

and letting go of the definitions and characteristics
  of objects:

these are the instructions of the Victorious One.

—CHAPTER 14

UP UNTIL this point we have dis-
cussed the cultivation, conduct, and
effort of a bodhisattva, which are the virtuous internal and
external conditions that support meditative practice. Now
it is time to learn the meditation of the Buddha. The root
text of the *King of Meditation Sutra* says that those who meditate skillfully will be joyous and free from physical pain.
They will naturally maintain their conduct, and their paths
will be free from obstacles. Finally, they will sustain the
view of the Buddha and will liberate themselves.

Whenever the Buddha speaks of the principles of
Mahayana meditation, he always mentions three pillars:
emptiness, the absence of characteristics, and wishlessness. We will discuss meditation in the context of these
three pillars.

Nagarjuna taught that emptiness goes beyond the four extremes of existence, nonexistence, both, and neither. If we believe something to be real and to have inherent substance, we are grasping at existence. If we believe that all is void, we fall into the extreme of nonexistence. To believe that appearances are both existent and nonexistent is still grasping at an extreme, and likewise to believe that objects are neither existent nor nonexistent is the final extreme. Emptiness transcends conceptual grasping altogether. Until we realize emptiness, we jump from one extreme to another.

Shakyamuni Buddha said that to sustain the view of emptiness is to become free from the effort of maintaining samadhi, yet to nonetheless remain in samadhi. There are essentially two stages within the practice of meditation that lead to this effortless sustaining. Our meditation practice first takes an object of support, then subsequently it does not. The Buddha teaches both of these stages in the *King of Meditation Sutra*.

1ST: VISUALIZE THE RADIANT BUDDHA

With his pure body of golden hue,
the lord of this world is magnificent.
A bodhisattva who focuses on this perception
is maintaining samadhi. . . .
Whoever brings to mind the form of the Tathagata
will have pacified senses and peace of mind.
His mind will always rest free of confusion.

—CHAPTER 4

We begin by visualizing the golden body of the Buddha and resting our attention upon that form. Imagine the Buddha appears in the sky before you upon a lotus throne. His shining body is immaculate—it is the most beautiful thing you have ever seen. Intentionally recollect his splendor. He is heavy and radiant with love and wisdom, and he directs his gaze at you. He is wide awake, free from judgment, compassionate, and omniscient. His wisdom light radiates out to you and to all beings. Endeavor in visualizing the Buddha, and the benefits will always follow you.

> By cultivating the mind stream in that way,
> you will see the protector of this world day
>   and night.
> When one day you become sick and unwell
> and experience the suffering of imminent death,
> your recollection of the buddha will not wane
> and you will not be overcome by the experience
>   of suffering.
> Thus, those who inquire with wisdom
> know all past and future phenomena to be empty,
> and, abiding in the way things are,
> they enjoy their practice and never tire.
>
> —CHAPTER 4

Sustain this visualization and recall that the blissful nature of the Buddha is not separate from your own nature. This nature is unconditioned and causeless. Nobody made this causeless nature.

The wise understand the conditioned and the
   unconditioned
and, repudiating the conception of causes,
they abide within the causeless.
Thus they know all phenomena to be empty.

—CHAPTER 4

2ND: DISSOLVE THE VISUALIZATION

Abiding within the recognition that the nature of the Buddha is your nature, sustain the visualization of the Buddha for some time. Then, dissolve his form into space. As soon as you dissolve the visualization, rest in ease without focusing on anything whatsoever. Simply rest. This is shamatha, or calm-abiding, without focus. When we develop the ability to rest in shamatha without focus, we are beginning the practice of emptiness.

Youthful Moon, bodhisattva mahasattvas who master the wisdom that all phenomena are by nature insubstantial do not get attached to any form, sound, smell, taste, sensation, or mental phenomenon. They do not have aversion to them. They are not ignorant with regards to them. Why is that?

They do not truly perceive these phenomena; they do not ascertain these phenomena. So what attachment could they possibly have? To what could they be attached? Who could be attached? What aversion could they have? What could they have aversion to? Who could have aversion? What ignorance could they have? What could they be ignorant about? Who is there to be ignorant? They do not truly perceive or ascertain any of these phenomena.

—CHAPTER 8

Resting in stable shamatha free from focus, ask yourself the question: "Who is holding this view?" Look for the observer. The observer is neither in nor out. When you cannot find where the observer arises, let go of looking. This is how to see the mind. This is called "the absence of characteristics." If you meditate in this way, the state of wishlessness comes naturally. You don't cling to the thought of enlightenment and you don't wish to be free from the lower realms. You have no hope and you have no fear. In this space, the empty nature will become apparent. When you see the empty nature, you see that form, sound, smell, taste, and touch are all empty. In the moment of seeing the empty nature, you have no desire, no anger, and no ignorance. In the moment of seeing, you will not see a single thing that has substantial existence. Do not cling.

When they are in the midst of a mountain forest,
people will sing, laugh, and cry out loud.
Though you hear these echoes, you pay them
  no heed.
Likewise, understand all phenomena to be this way.

—CHAPTER 9

3RD: IN POST-MEDITATION, EVERYTHING IS ILLUSION

Imagine you are alone in a mountain forest. All is quiet and clear and fresh. Drifting through the trees, you hear people laughing and talking and crying. You do not see the people, but the sound comes nonetheless. When you look for the sound—where it arises, where it abides, and where it goes—you cannot find it. It is mere sound, without basis. All phenomena are like this. Examine sounds this very moment. Where do they arise, where do they abide, where do they go?

> When the moon rises in a clear sky
> and its reflection appears in a clear lake,
> the moon did not enter the water.
> Likewise, understand all phenomena to be defined
>   in this way.
>
> —CHAPTER 9

In an utterly clear sky, you see the bright moon. Before you is a placid lake with not a single ripple stirring its surface. You look into the lake and there is the moon again. The moon did not come down and settle in the lake. It is only a reflection. All phenomena are like this reflection. Consider this and then look at appearances. Maybe you have heard this metaphor before? Do not leave it as a mere thought now but look freshly at what appears. Look and see how everything is like the moon in the lake.

Through the power of insight, which comes from training in meditation again and again, you witness nothing actually present within the appearances of our world. You don't fabricate the experience of phenomena being insubstantial, nor do you overlay "nothingness" onto the world. You look with the power of increasing insight and see that all *is* like the moon in the clear lake. This is why we say that everything is emptiness, peace, and stainless from the beginning. What is there to be stained?

In the same way, a practitioner who desires to attain samadhi observes how the three poisons of attachment, aversion, and ignorance are dependent on the six objects of the senses. You see a pleasing form, and you experience desire. You hear a harsh sound or smell a repulsive odor, and you feel anger or aversion. When you meet the objects of form, sound, smell, taste, feeling, and phenomenal experience, you engage the continuity of karma. If you see the illusory nature of these objects, you will not be attached to them, and you will not perpetuate the cycle of samsara. Likewise, when you cannot find the desiring self, the angry self, or the ignorant self, then samsara untangles. This is how samadhi dawns.

> Youthful Moon, how is it that bodhisattva mahasattvas master the essential wisdom of the insubstantiality of all phenomena? Youth, bodhisattva mahasattvas need to fully know that all phenomena are substanceless, essenceless, uncharacterized, undefined, unborn, unceasing, unwritten, empty, primordially peaceful, and naturally pure.
>
> —CHAPTER 8

The Buddha says that whoever really practices insight meditation will not become stirred. They will be careful; they will recall the Buddha. They will maintain their conduct, and their wisdom will not flicker in and out. They will not abandon the Dharma, and they will always tame their mind in the correct way.

The true nature is empty, it is peace, and from the beginning it is stainless. Whoever realizes this and is never separate from this realization, we call a buddha. Whoever sees phenomena to be naturally untainted from the beginning, we call a buddha. A buddha has let go of all extremes.

> Both "existence" and "nonexistence" are extremes,
> just as purity and impurity are extremes as well.
> Therefore, letting go of both types of extremes,
> the wise do not remain in the middle either.
>
> —CHAPTER 9

We cannot dwell in the extremes of existence and nonexistence, pure and impure, good and bad. But we should not remain stuck in the middle either, because that is also a position to which one clings. When we hold any position at all, we are entering into debate with other positions. As long as the tension of a position remains, we suffer. When we don't have a position to defend, either through internal debate or debate with others, our suffering dwindles.

In the realization of emptiness, there is no conceptual thought. There are no objects to cling to. The appearances of the world are not truly established. That is the samadhi.

One day, while meditating with the intention to realize this nature for the benefit of all beings, the subtle conceit of there being a meditator who is meditating will fall away altogether. That is the samadhi.

It is not possible for a normal being to be born with no fear. However, over the course of a single life, one can attain fearlessness. Fearlessness comes from wishlessness, which comes from abandoning pretense or conceit. It is possible to speak very eloquently about the Buddha's teachings, meditate very diligently, and investigate the mind continuously with the intention to become liberated, yet still maintain conceit.

> Even as they talk about the four noble truths,
> the immature claim, "I see the truth."
> There can be no conceit in seeing the truth:
> the Victorious One said truth is without conceit.
> —CHAPTER 9

Immature people may say, "I saw the truth," but in saying so they are grasping at it. The truth is actually the absence of grasping. If you grasp at having seen the truth, then you are no longer seeing the truth. Some people think they understand many teachings and are proud of hearing so much Dharma, but they never keep their discipline. Because they break their discipline, they descend into the lower realms. What you hear does not save you, and what you say about the truth does not save you. Once you completely rest in the absence of clinging, samadhi will dawn.

4TH: ALLOW FOR REALIZATION

Once you rest in meditation
without believing in anything,
this state devoid of any pretense
is known as samadhi.

—CHAPTER 13

There are two kinds of conceit. The first relates to view, and the second relates to conduct. The first conceit is to hold the thought, "My view is superior to your view." If you think in this way, your view cannot be superior. The second conceit is to become inflated by the purity of your own conduct. If you are inflated, you haven't attained the ultimate discipline. If you don't study much and you don't listen much, but you become so proud of your rigorous discipline, you are bound to fall from your proud heights. In this world, there are many meditators, but they do not reduce their ego-clinging at all. Consequently, negative emotions arise in them, again and again. These practitioners do not understand selflessness and do not apply the meditation that sees the empty nature. When they do, they will attain nirvana.

Once these types of conceit fall away, you become a spiritual medicine for the world. You become a treasury of wisdom with boundless dignity. You become open and generous. When you encounter people without support, you effortlessly become their support. You become the vessel that brings people to the shore of awakening. You become the answer.

What is the answer? It is the Dharma. You become the Dharma. Your mouth is the source from which words of truth flow. If you don't have realization, the Dharma doesn't issue forth from you—cannot issue forth from you—and your words lack power. The provisional words of the teachings are sacred, but even more sacred are the words that spring forth from an enlightened being as he or she moves through the world—words that are perfectly suited to your current situation the moment they issue forth.

If the Buddha hadn't attained realization, then the Dharma would not have flowed forth from his mouth. We turn toward the Buddha because the Buddha is the source of the Dharma. If you connect with the realization that radiates from the Buddha, you become the Buddha in that moment, and all buddhas praise you. When you sit in connection with that realization, countless buddhas bless you. This is an overwhelming feeling.

This realization is not a state of absorption. It is nonmeditation, arising from the supportive conditions of making offerings, visualization, meditation, ethical conduct, and correct view. It is training in the nature. This nature is the *dharmakaya*, the ultimate state of the Buddha.

> Those who abide in the dharmakaya
> know all entities to be insubstantial.
> Unraveling the perception of entities,
> they do not see the form bodies of the buddha.
> —CHAPTER 4

Training in the nature comes down to resting in the sky-like dharmakaya. This is what we call nonmeditation. Right and wrong, good and bad—the whole dualistic function of mind is abandoned. From meditation without focus, we gain the capacity for nonmeditation. We gain the capacity to just sit in the essential nature. We don't retract the senses. If you sit like this, you are not abiding within the mind that discriminates and parses experience. When you leave the senses wide open and naturally sustain the absence of clinging, all things that appear are ornaments of the dharmakaya. Most of the time, we experience samsara, but when we sit like this, the mind itself is luminous.

> Youth, the qualities of the buddha are infinite, inconceivable, unthinkable, unimaginable, immeasurable. Why is that? Youth, the nature of mind is formless and undefinable. Youth, that nature of mind is the essence of the Buddha's qualities. The essence of the Buddha's qualities is the essence of the tathagatas. The essence of the tathagatas is the essence of all phenomena.
>
> —CHAPTER 12

The *Wisdom of the Time of Death Sutra* says that when the mind realizes itself, it is wisdom. Do not search for the Buddha elsewhere. When you realize the empty nature of the mind, that is the moment of knowing buddha, the awakened state that is indivisible from Shakyamuni Buddha and that is the essence of all phenomena.

This meditation eliminates attachment, liberates aversion, and is beyond ignorance. When you start to meditate in this way, you surpass ignorance and the source of samsaric struggle. We all innately have this wisdom. We must simply unfold it.

I must say again that in order to practice this profound meditation that is nonmeditation, many conditions must come together. If we just try to sit and rest in the mind's nature, we throw ourselves against an invisible wall and we won't achieve the result we wish for. The Buddha teaches us here, in this text, how to bring about the conditions that lead to realizing emptiness. So, assemble all of the conditions! Then, place your mind on the form of the Buddha, dissolve the form, and rest in calm-abiding without focus. When you effortlessly see the mind's nature, that is the great seal of the dharmakaya, that is the great understanding.

> The fruition of the mind
> that rests in meditation
> has the same character, name, and form;
> these are pure and luminous.
> —CHAPTER 18

Awakening to Victorious Meditation

Developing Shamatha by Visualizing the Buddha

1. Train in maintaining a clear and steady visualization of the form of the Buddha. He is golden-hued, heavy with love and wisdom, and he directs his transcendent eyes at you. Feel the presence of the Buddha and the ceaseless blessings he bestows.

2. Dissolve the visualization into space by shrinking the form of the Buddha until it is completely gone.

3. Rest in shamatha, calm-abiding, without focusing on anything.

4. Endeavor in this practice until you have developed stable shamatha without a focus. This will take many practice sessions. Once you have developed stability in this, begin to connect with the natural buddha, as instructed below.

Connecting with the Natural Buddha

Proceed through the visualization and recollection of the Buddha's wisdom-presence, just as stated above. Remind yourself that the Buddha before you is always present and is never separate from the nature of your mind. The Buddha slowly shrinks, but instead of dissolving into space, he melts into light and then dissolves into you. Then, rest in the state of knowing that you are never separate from the Buddha's nature.

Within this resting state:

1. Whatever thoughts arise within your mind, their very nature is empty.

2. When looking at the awareness of that, it is also empty.

3. Rest without grasping.

Enhance your practice in the following ways:

- Make offerings to the Buddha, Dharma, and Sangha.

- Practice the visualization of the Buddha continuously in order to enhance the transcendent dignity that knows you are never separate from the Buddha.

- Develop compassion through training in all aspects of the path.

11

WISDOM
THE INCONCEIVABLE BUDDHA

On the surface of one hair dwell all five classes of beings—
hell beings, creatures of the animal realm,
beings from the realms of ghosts, gods, and humans,
who do not mingle or interfere with each other.
In their worlds are lakes and oceans,
rivers, ponds, and springs—
nor do these mingle or interfere with each other.
That is how inconceivable the Buddhadharma is.

—CHAPTER 19

1ST: PHENOMENA ARE
ACTUALLY PURE AND INFINITE

ON A SINGLE hair, lakes and oceans abide without touching. Within every single conceptualized fragment of space there are hells of heat and cold, there are thousands of beings enjoying the bliss of the gods, and there are thousands of buddha realms with beings practicing meditation and experiencing the wisdom that goes beyond obscuration. In these buddha realms there are noble ones teaching and sitting, seeming to appear, and seeming to disappear. There is not one buddha—there are infinite buddhas. If you don't have transcendent wisdom, you will not see in this way.

> On the surface of one hair there are as many buddhas
> as there are grains of sand in the Ganga river,
> and these victorious ones have just as many
>   pure lands
> of various kinds and characteristics.
>
> —CHAPTER 18

If one has pure perception, every single part of the body is the Buddha. Whatever we see is buddha. Sometimes people who are not practicing pure perception will question the validity and source of our methods. This description offered by the Buddha in the *King of Meditation Sutra* establishes the foundation for the way that we begin to practice pure perception.

> Just as the Buddha's awakening,
> so are his attributes.
> Just as his attributes,
> so is his body.
> Just as his body, awakening, and attributes,
> so are the Buddha's pure lands;
> and his powers, liberation, and meditation
> are also of a single character.
>
> —CHAPTER 18

The realization, body, and pure lands of every buddha share the same nature, and all that appears and exists within our experience is also of that nature. Recognizing that everything will eventually become pure within our experience allows us to make fearless aspirations. Along the path, we make the aspiration that we may one day descend into the hell realms to teach beings the sublime Dharma that liberates from suffering. The Indian Buddhist master Shantideva said that bodhisattvas descend to the hell realms like swans landing on placid lakes. We too should make the wish to carry out this type of activity, knowing that as bodhisattvas we will see the appearances of the hells as pure.

> Know all phenomena to be illusory;
> like the sky is naturally empty,
> know their nature to be just so.
> Practicing this, you will be attached to nothing;
> with detached wisdom, you will bring benefit;
> though of this world, you will engage in supreme
>   awakened activity.
> —CHAPTER 11

There is a traditional story of five blind men who are trying to determine the shape of an elephant. One man holds the trunk and says that an elephant is long. The second holds the tail and says that it is small. Another runs his hands over the stomach and describes it as round and rough. They each try to describe the elephant, but each man only relates to a small part of the large animal. Similarly, the teachings express the nature of the Buddha to sentient beings who have never seen it. Some say it is emptiness, some say it is selflessness, and some say it is pure perception. What is it really? These words describe the nature of buddha, but the buddha is the dharmata, the essence of reality that is beyond intellectual comprehension and beyond description. And yet the inconceivability of the dharmata does not hinder the descriptive teachings. The buddha is both beyond and inseparable from the teachings.

2ND: FORM AND AWAKENING ARE NOT SEPARATE

Form and awakening are equivalent:
you will find nothing to differentiate them.
Even as you explain nirvana
through words in a profound way,
nirvana will not be found,
nor will you find its name.
Neither of them can be found.
Thus, all empty phenomena
are taught to be nirvana.

—CHAPTER 25

We should not speak of an awakening that occurs separate from form. All things arise in dependence upon all other things. You cannot say that a tangerine is its own entity.

It is the result of a seed, soil, water, sun, and wind. To apprehend a tangerine is dependent upon the people who brought it to where it is now and the countless elements that hold it together. It depends upon the eye that perceives, the object perceived, and consciousness. When you look closely into the appearance of anything, the ultimate truth is just there. No object exists as a separate entity from anything else. Nagarjuna said that it is precisely because everything is emptiness that anything is possible. Anything that is conditioned is naturally empty of an independent, unchanging existence.

In the Vajrayana, we teach that all phenomena are the deity. When we hear this, doubt might arise. How can these impure appearances be the deity? But if we understand the Mahayana view that everything is conditioned and therefore empty, we can move into the understanding that everything is primordially enlightened. Through accumulating merit and wisdom it becomes possible to see this. When we see this, we gain immense flexibility to see whatever we wish.

Visualizing a "conceivable" buddha helps us make the leap to the inconceivable buddha, who is apparent as the nature of all form. Some New Age individuals will hear this and think they can imagine whatever they want and call that the Buddha. Or they will think they can visualize Buddha Shakyamuni in a three-piece suit, giving teachings to all sentient beings. On one hand, of course you can do this. Everything that appears *is* a reflection of Buddha-nature, so you *can* say that anything you visualize reflects the Buddha. The question is: Does this actually lead to realization or just to more concepts?

Does visualizing Shakyamuni Buddha in a three-piece suit help you connect with the qualities of the awakened state as much as visualizing a radiant buddha in Dharma robes, ablaze with wisdom light? If not, and you are visualizing this way simply to exercise your free will, then you are actually being self-indulgent and unskillful. Dharma means coming to understand your nature, not playing with mental potential. We can become infatuated with our own methods and actually misuse our mind's potential. Practice always comes back to sincerity, to developing the mind, to benefiting others. When we enter into more advanced visualization practices, we realize that the features of the Buddha hold a potent symbolic power for helping us realize the ultimate dharmakaya buddha. Visualizing the Buddha holding an iPad does not give us access to wisdom in the same way that visualizing a nectar-filled alms bowl does. The traditional symbols of the Buddha correspond to qualities present within awakened mind—they have power.

As we wade into the conceptual understanding that appearances are the empty essence, we will get involved in many angles of intellectual inquiry. Questions like "If appearances are impermanent, is the Buddha impermanent?" are often debated in monastic settings. The more we penetrate the meaning of these questions through study and discussion, the more we clarify our understanding of Buddha. The clearer our conventional understanding, the easier it is to access the inconceivable Buddha. However, remember that the point of inquiry is to gain the confidence to move beyond conceptual elaboration altogether.

Here is another angle: form and the Buddha are the same in essence, but their expression is different. What you see right now is relative. What the mind's nature sees is the mind's nature. When you say "right," you seem to exclude "left," and vice versa. But actually, "left" and "right" are inseparable. Which one came first? Did the concept of "right" emerge before the concept of "left?" In actuality, these concepts arise at the same time. They are dependent on each other. Similarly, if you want to understand how form and the enlightened nature are inseparable, you need to see the way you either fixate on form or fixate on the subtle *idea* of emptiness. Both are fixation. Fixation on concepts prevents us from resolving the inseparability that is beyond concepts. We must allow judgment to collapse naturally in order to see the Buddha that is not separate from form.

> If bodhisattva mahasattvas possess this one characteristic, they will obtain these qualities and swiftly, fully accomplish unsurpassable, perfect, and complete awakening. What is this one characteristic? Youthful Moon, it is bodhisattva mahasattvas' knowledge of the essence of all phenomena. Youthful Moon, how can bodhisattva mahasattvas know the essence of all phenomena? Youthful Moon, bodhisattva mahasattvas know that the

names of phenomena do not exist and that phenomena have no name. They know all phenomena to be soundless, wordless, without inscription, birthless, and ceaseless. Their causes and properties are in discord, and their conditions and properties are in discord. They are defined by isolation. Their unique characteristic is to be uncharacterized. They have no characteristics. They are inconceivable, unthinkable, and beyond mind.

—CHAPTER 11

3RD: SUSPEND JUDGMENT

When we practice suspending judgment, we decrease grasping, and the dualistic mind loses its rigidity. Right now, we experience endless dualism. The dualistic mind cannot apprehend the nondual union of form and emptiness. Only by giving rise to the nondual mind can nondual experience unfold. No matter how much we think about nonduality, we will not experience it unless we walk a path that leads us to suspend conceptuality altogether.

The wisdom that sees like this is what allows you to actually practice the six paramitas well. With transcendent wisdom, you know how to give generously but without attachment in the process of giving. You are never separate from discipline, but you neither accept nor reject. You have unceasing patience, but you do not cling to sentient beings. You have powerful motivation to practice, but your body and mind never grasp at a self-centered outcome. You maintain the practice of meditation, but you don't maintain the concept of meditation.

When you practice in this way, obstacles cannot touch you. Being interrogated by skeptics will not cause you to doubt your view. You will have great compassion. You will not be enticed by the narrower aims of those who strive only to realize the absence of a personal self but not the insubstantiality of all phenomena. When you bring this transcendent wisdom into the practice of the six paramitas, you gain the victorious samadhi of the Buddha. Through this samadhi, you actualize the four discerning awarenesses.

> Bodhisattva mahasattvas think in the following way: "I wish to actualize the four discerning awarenesses by all means possible." What are these four? They are the awarenesses that correctly discern the Dharma, objects, language, and eloquence.
>
> —CHAPTER 24

We are often skeptical when we hear the Buddha described as "omniscient." Omniscience here doesn't mean that the Buddha knows how to make cranberry juice. It means he has realized the nature of everything that could possibly arise—he has realized the nature of every being that has ever come in the past and will ever come in the future. This is why we call the Buddha omniscient. It really doesn't matter whether the Buddha can make cranberry juice. Cranberry juice doesn't solve our problems.

When you understand the relative function of the five

aggregates of form, feeling, perception, formation, and consciousness, you have correct understanding. Everyone possesses these five aggregates. Therefore, if you understand how your own aggregates work, you know the function of another person's constituents and you can "discern phenomena" correctly. After you have understood how the aggregates work, you can go deeper to see their nature. If you arrive at the understanding of their nature, you have comprehended the "meaning" correctly. When you can precisely explain this meaning, your speech is called "definitive word." What arises from these three—the discernment of phenomena, the understanding of meaning, and definitive word—is "confidence." You gain confidence in your own understanding, in your ability to eloquently express the teachings, and in knowing that the person who is listening has understood. You are then able to express the Dharma.

Only completely enlightened buddhas possess the full power of the four discerning awarenesses. The awarenesses emerge from the unobscured nature of the Buddha. In order for bodhisattvas to gain these awarenesses, they continuously train in the great samadhi.

> However many faults conditioned phenomena
>   may have,
> there are as many praises to be made for nirvana.
>   —CHAPTER 24

4TH: REMEMBER THE BUDDHA IS DHARMAKAYA

Samsara is constituted by endless formations. These impermanent formations are always stained by grasping, and therefore always accompanied by suffering. Can any sentient being understand the extent of these endless formations? Can any samsaric being know everything that is unfolding, not just within this world, but throughout the vast universe of countless worlds? Of course not—these formations are endless. When we recognize that we cannot conceive of all formations, we understand how nirvana, which conquers and therefore surpasses all of the phenomena of samsara, is inconceivable. From here we can relate to the inconceivability of the awakened state.

Do not consider the ultimate buddha to be the *rupakaya*, the "form body." The ultimate Buddha is dharmakaya, the "truth body," free from characteristics. It is immeasurable and unmoving—it is like space. Whether there is bliss or suffering, dharmakaya does not change. Dharmakaya is emptiness. Beings who want to hear the language of the Buddha's wisdom should know that the Buddha's wisdom is beyond language. People with the desire to achieve buddhahood must know that the Buddha is beyond even that desire.

You and I may look at a statue of the Buddha and see similar appearances. We can both speak of the *ushnisha* at the Buddha's crown, or the golden color of his body, but we do not see those features in the same way. We have strong overlapping karma, as we are both humans in this particular place and time. We see similarities due to the power of our similar conditioning, but the teachings never say that we see the same thing. The Buddha does not have an objective form.

> It is not easy to understand the Tathagata's body in terms of characteristics and actions. He can be of blue color . . . yellow color . . .
>
> —CHAPTER 18

While humans almost always have a similar perception of the form of the Buddha, the exact same perception is impossible. Therefore, the rupakaya is a reflection of the dharmakaya, and it appears in accordance with the karma of individual beings. As it is said in the sutra:

> Youthful Moon, therefore, the body of the Tathagata is pure. It cannot be thought of in terms of impure characteristics. It is taught to be inconceivable. It cannot be characterized in any way.
>
> —CHAPTER 18

In the foundational Buddhist teachings, we find a standard representation of the historical Buddha. This relates to a limited perception of the Buddha—one that doesn't include an understanding of the form body and the truth body. In the Mahayana, this view is expanded, and in the Vajrayana, it is completely revealed. We see buddhas in countless forms, in various shapes, some even with pig's heads. Why is this? The form of a pig is also a reflection of the essential nature, and it is therefore ultimately Buddha.

Approaching the Inconceivable

Rupakaya Practice

1. Develop the visualization of the Buddha in front of you, as indicated in the preceding chapter on meditation. Now, enhance your understanding by reminding yourself that all appearances are not separate from the Buddha. Intentionally bring *everything* into inseparability with the form visualized in front of you.

2. Then, understand that the Buddha is not separate from all the appearances around you. Expand the essence of the Buddha's form outward into all appearances.

3. Oscillate between reminding yourself that all phenomena are inseparable from the Buddha and that the Buddha pervades all phenomena.

Dharmakaya Practice

Begin with the rupakaya practice of visualizing the Buddha. Maintain the visualization of the form of the Buddha, and instantly resolve everything as being already the nature of dharmakaya, the empty essence. Without needing to dissolve the Buddha or conceptually reconcile anything whatsoever, close the gap between the dharmakaya and the rupakaya.

This practice is difficult and will take a long time to develop. The result is confidence, an absence of doubt, and the dignity of knowing that your nature is enlightened. To be without doubt is to know exactly what to do. To have confidence is to enjoy and trust the practice. Dignity ensues when the trust has moved into experience.

You know you have gained insight when the six paramitas are inseparable from the Buddha. When you offer money to someone on the street, you don't cling to that person as an entity but experience the inseparability of the nature of everything.

12

The Treasure of Awakening

1st: Awakening Is Rich

As the Buddha placed his foot upon the threshold at
    the gate,
all were freed from hunger and thirst.
As the Buddha placed his foot upon the threshold at
    the gate,
all those who were blind,
who were deaf, or helpless, or had little merit—
obtained eyes and ears.
As the Buddha placed his foot upon the threshold
    at the gate,
whatever hungry ghosts were dwelling in the underworld—
suffering while eating mucus and spit—
were touched by light, were put at ease.
As the Buddha placed his foot upon the threshold
    at the gate,
cliff tops, mountain summits,
all precious sala trees, karnikara trees, and the like
bowed in the direction of the Buddha.

—CHAPTER 10

WE SOMETIMES hear that the Buddha has no power—that he can teach, but we must do all of the work ourselves. This is the view held by the followers of early Buddhism. In the Mahayana, we understand how the Buddha is endowed with inconceivable abilities and has the power to benefit us.

When consciousness is liberated from everything, one sees the nature of the mind. At that moment, wisdom arises. We are not talking about a worldly understanding. We are talking about *wisdom.* We are talking about that which is most powerful and brings complete freedom in all activity. When samadhi is improved and eventually perfected, one can go to countless pure fields of experience and meet oceans of buddhas. This is the kind of potential that is completely beyond our comprehension. A statement like this will draw criticism from one who is entrenched in the conditioning of language, culture, and, in short, samsara—none of which is able to approach this potential. But the more we study and practice, the more we will connect to this capacity—not out of blind faith, but by seeing what the Buddha actually is.

The body of the Buddha does not have a single form. The Buddha manifests out of compassion in accordance with the needs of beings. The Buddha does not have gender, though at particular times we may refer to the form of a buddha as "him" or "her." The Buddha is not a man or a woman, does not have a particular color or size, and does not exist in a particular direction. The appearance of the Buddha in relative experience depends upon the conditioning and needs of each sentient being.

It is said that whoever wants to know the *kayas,* the bodies of the Buddha, must practice the sublime samadhi. One who practices this samadhi sees how the thirty-two major and eighty minor qualities of the Buddha's body are actually the same as unconditioned awakening.

In the Vajrayana, we speak of the five kayas, the five speeches, the five hearts, the five wisdoms, the five qualities, and the five activities. When we speak of the five qualities, we sometimes talk about the throne of the deity, where the Buddha resides. We say that this quality, this throne, exists primordially within the pure nature.

If we maintain the realization of the empty nature, we maintain all of the powers and qualities of the Buddha. Buddha-fields, which are inseparable from the mind's nature, unfold wherever there is a buddha. If we maintain this realization, pure compassion radiates outward to all sentient beings.

2ND: SUSTAIN THE TREASURE OF SAMADHI

Wearing the armor of great Dharma,
the strong and brave
are struck by the ultimate *vajra* of emptiness
with which they then strike.

—CHAPTER 33

One who maintains this nature is like a priceless treasure. One of my gurus, Tulku Urgyen Rinpoche, told me that if you rest in the authentic samadhi for a single second it generates more merit than making countless offerings to all the buddhas and bodhisattvas.

> Whoever upholds
> this peerless, immaculate samadhi
> is like the boundless wealth of the buddhas,
> a vast ocean of wisdom.
> —CHAPTER 37

The *King of Meditation Sutra* says the first quality of a bodhisattva who holds the profound samadhi is that she cannot be outshone—she becomes like the sun or like the waxing moon among the stars. Second, she who holds this samadhi is unshakeable. Anyone who interrogates her cannot conquer her position because she has sublime insight. The third quality is that the wisdom of such a person is immeasurable. She can answer any question with skill. The fourth quality, my favorite, is that her confidence, her dignity, becomes immovable.

Samadhi is not just a stable mind. Samadhi is the flowing forth of wisdom that grants the four treasures of the Buddha, the Dharma, wisdom, and knowing the three times (past, present, and future).

The treasure of the Buddha is the power of vision, the power of hearing, and the power to know the minds of others. It is the knowing of past lives and future lives and gaining mastery over miraculous powers.

The treasure of the Dharma is the ability to hear all of the Buddha's teachings wherever they are taught. Those with this ability are so perceptive, with hearing so transcendent, that they can actually listen to the teachings resounding in the ten directions. They are never separate from the Buddha's teachings.

The treasure of wisdom is just that—great wisdom. One understands everything and is beyond the concept of "forgetting." Beings with this treasure are able to teach others and precisely know the meaning of all teachings.

The treasure of knowing the three times is also exactly that: one sees the minds and conduct of sentient beings in the past, present, and future.

When one holds these four treasures, one's activity on behalf of others becomes infinite. If you make a strong effort not to break your vows, are persistent in your practice, and listen to the teachings of the sutras, you cannot help but gain these treasures. By holding the meaning of this sutra in your body, speech, and mind, you will give rise to enlightened dignity. No action can compete with the benefit of having made the determination to adhere to even a single line of the sutra. The Buddha says all of this in the root text. So feel fortunate, practice accumulating and dedicating, and be persistent in upholding the intent of the sutra. Then you will gain confidence.

Motivating Yourself with the Treasures

Motivate yourself by contemplating the qualities of the buddhas. Say to yourself, "I must practice." Think that all the enlightened qualities mentioned are perfected and innate within the realization of the essential nature. This realization is samadhi. Contemplate your completely clean and awakened Buddha-nature.

13
UPHOLDING THE TEACHINGS

It is rare for a buddha to have appeared in this world.
Rebirth as a human being is scarce,
as is faith in the teachings, renunciation, and ordination.
Whoever makes dedications for the mind of awakening
is pleasing to our guide.

—CHAPTER 25

To be born in a place where a buddha has appeared is extremely difficult. Among the countless insects, animals, and formless beings, to be a human is quite rare. To truly practice the Dharma is even more rare, and to dedicate the virtue that you've gathered for the sake of enlightenment is precious. We are therefore very lucky. We should acknowledge our great merit and feel the preciousness of these temporary conditions.

If we dedicate our virtue while remembering the preciousness of this opportunity to practice, the buddhas are delighted. Remembering the points set forth in this sutra, we will not abandon our vows—we will practice well and maintain our conduct. Although we dedicate at the end of sessions or after having accumulated virtue, a continuous sense of dedication can carry us along the path.

The Buddha said that anyone who upholds the *King of Meditation Sutra* will develop great dignity. He said that through hearing only four lines of the sutra, one gathers more merit than could be spoken of. The Buddha also said that upholding in our practice even a single line of this sutra gathers more merit than respectfully offering countless gifts to the noble ones. We should therefore uphold as much of what is taught in the sutra as we can and dedicate the generosity of our efforts in four ways.

> Bodhisattva mahasattvas also dedicate their generosity in four ways. What are these four?
>
> "May I generate the roots of the virtue of generosity in order to obtain the skillful means through which the blessed ones actualized unsurpassable, perfect, and complete awakening." This is the first dedication.
>
> "May I generate the roots of the virtue of generosity so that I may always be accompanied by spiritual teachers who will help me to accomplish unsurpassable, perfect, and complete awakening, as I learn, memorize, understand, recite, and maintain their teachings about skillful means under their guidance." This is the second dedication.
>
> "May I generate the roots of the virtue of generosity so that I may acquire wealth that can bring sustenance to the entire world." This is the third dedication.

"May I generate the roots of the virtue of generosity so I become accomplished in this very life, and so that this body may become source of the two types of benefit, as I help beings through the Dharma and through material aid." This is the fourth dedication.

—CHAPTER 35

Great beings make four dedications after completing their practice or after giving generously. First, they dedicate their merit to learning the methods that lead to realization. In this way, they plant the seeds of future learning and turn the momentum of their practice toward acquiring samadhi.

Second, which I find to be particularly important, bodhisattvas make the aspiration to have an authentic teacher who will always hold and protect them, who will teach them to practice correctly, and who will guide them along the path.

Third, they dedicate and aspire to gain the very practical conditions of correct livelihood and material support that make it easier to practice. This means being supported by clean money and clean resources. It is necessary to remember this dedication.

The fourth dedication is made with the aspiration to give rise to generosity—the generosity of material things and the generosity of the Dharma. This dedication shows that the Dharma of Shakyamuni Buddha is not in conflict with living in the world.

Some people criticize Buddhists, saying nonsensical

things like, "Oh, they only practice for enlightenment, and they don't care about others." This thought is completely wrong. Complete and total enlightenment is impossible to gain without the wish to be an active force of benefit for others. The very movement outward to other beings, the bodhichitta that expansively embraces everyone, is the core of the path. Offering the Dharma that will lead beings into virtue means actually planting the seeds for a noble society.

> Whichever learned person offers the Dharma
> is always abiding by the Dharma of great beings.
> His country, too, will become pure and virtuous
> and conditions conducive to awakening will flourish.
>
> —CHAPTER 29

Imagine you are a good practitioner. You have pure motivation, you have given rise to bodhichitta and therefore see all beings as equal, and you really want to offer the truth to all beings. If you want to be able to bring Dharma to all beings, you have to sit with Dharma yourself. Without abiding in Dharma, you cannot transmit Dharma. When you truly begin to offer Dharma from the place of Dharma, everything is transformed into purity. The person receiving your offering, yourself, all perceptions—everything becomes increasingly purified.

But please remember that to offer the Dharma truly, you must pay homage to your teachers and reduce your pride. In that way you lay the groundwork to begin to benefit others through teaching the Dharma.

Extending words of respect to their teachers
and eliminating pride from the start—
this is how the victorious lords of Dharma teach.
Their minds are only stirred by virtue;
they have understood and realized wisdom.
They always abandon ignorant tendencies
and teach the factors of supreme awakening.

—CHAPTER 14

Through engaging in such conduct, you will begin to develop a lot of merit. For example, some teachers tell me that they improve more through teaching others than by practicing alone. I believe this can be the case, because while teaching they need a strong motivation to offer the Dharma purely. When one offers this Dharma purely, powerful qualities arise.

Youthful Moon, you should know that bodhisattva mahasattvas who retain, understand, uphold, read, recite, transmit, chant, and extensively teach this samadhi to others obtain four beneficial qualities. What are these four? Their merit cannot be outshone, they are unassailable by opponents, their wisdom is immeasurable, and their confidence is unlimited.

—CHAPTER 18

Of course, there are also fake teachers. One may try to offer the Dharma to others without personally actually abiding in the Dharma of the Buddha. The Buddha prophesied the spreading of this type of hypocrisy in our current age.

> In the name of my teachings, they will ordain
> for the sake of sustaining their livelihoods.
> Overpowered by gain and honor,
> they will disparage one another.
>
> —CHAPTER 18

But now I speak of a good person brimming with bodhichitta, someone who loves the Dharma and is compassionate. If you are such a person, decent and endowed with the power to give the Dharma, you possess a very precious gift. A person who offers the Dharma increases their own enlightened qualities. There is genuine benefit for the one who offers and the one who receives. Therefore, offer this profound Dharma, which leads to the end of suffering.

> Bodhisattva mahasattvas who wish to swiftly achieve unsurpassable, perfect, and complete awakening and wish to liberate all beings from the ocean of samsara must listen to this King of Samadhi That Fully Reveals the Equal Nature of All Things, which is praised by all the buddhas and is the mother of all tathagatas. They must retain it, uphold it, understand it, read it, recite it, transmit it, chant it, and cultivate it through meditation free from afflictive emotions.
>
> —CHAPTER 9

Many of us know the old saying: "Give a man a fish and you feed him for a day. Teach a man to fish and you feed him for a lifetime." It is better to empower someone to thrive through knowledge than to let them scrounge for sustenance day by day. Likewise, if you give money and material things, you only help people for a short period of time, which is nonetheless a very good thing to do. But if, with pure motivation, you give someone the knowledge of Dharma, that knowledge will continue with the person until their enlightenment. When you give the Dharma, you benefit countless beings. Giving the knowledge that leads to enlightenment is greater than anything else you might give. When you give the words of the Buddha, you give the roots of all that is wholesome.

> The Buddha's words always dispel afflictive
>   emotions.
> They give rise to delight, without delight in
>   attachment;
> they give rise to loving-kindness without aversion;
> they give rise to wisdom without ignorance.
> The Buddha's words clear away all defilements.
> —CHAPTER 14

When we teach the *King of Meditation*, we give people the means to be free from the sickness of samsara, but we also give them the ability to be free from myriad other sicknesses of the world. Nowadays, scientists are conducting extensive research into the benefits of meditation on the cellular level, on our neurological systems, and on our hormonal systems. More than two thousand years ago, the Buddha described meditation as a way to alleviate all sickness—relative and ultimate. The Buddha is the doctor of beings, his teaching is the medicine, and the noble ones who uphold his teachings are like the nurses and caretakers who nurture you from sickness into health. The refuge offered by these three jewels is simply true and undeceiving.

We live within an ocean of sentient beings—moving, talking, sitting, sleeping, drinking coffee, driving cars, loving, and crying. We must hold this samadhi within the vast expanse of moving mind. If we persistently train in refining our understanding of reality, cultivating love and compassion, making offerings, engaging in proper conduct, and in meditation, and if we yearn for the highest wisdom, we will find no difficulty in seeing the Buddha. If we uphold this teaching with humbleness, dignity, and correct view, we will shine like Youthful Moon.

Dedication

This is the easiest way to dedicate:

> May the temple of sublime Dharma spread and
> flourish!
> May infinite sentient beings be happy and well!
> May samsara and the three lower realms be emptied
> and extinguished!
> May the hordes of maras be pacified and tamed!
> May I fulfill the aspirations of all bodhisattvas
> residing on the *bhumis*!

The sky can fall with its moon and stars,

the ground can crumble with its mountains and towns,

and outer space can transform its appearance,

but you never speak false words.

—CHAPTER 13

ABOUT THE AUTHOR

KYABGON PHAKCHOK Rinpoche was born in 1981 and is a lineage holder of the Profound Treasures of Chokgyur Lingpa from the Nyingma School of Tibetan Buddhism. He is also one of the heads of the Riwoche Taklung Kagyu lineage. Phakchok Rinpoche's primary root teachers are his grandfather, the late Kyabje Tulku Urgyen Rinpoche, as well as the late Dzogchen master Kyabje Nyoshul Khen Rinpoche.

Phakchok Rinpoche is a householder with a family, yet is responsible for several important monastic institutions. His life exemplifies the fine balance that many practitioners must find in today's world. According to the tradition we must study and contemplate to discern the profound meaning of the Buddha's teachings. We must practice in a way that genuinely reduces self-cherishing and negative emotions. We must engage in altruistic activity as the expression of our practice to help our community and beyond. This formula of study, contemplation, practice, and altruistic activity is what Rinpoche follows and teaches.

Rinpoche upholds the teachings of both Sutra and Mantra vehicles. As the vajra master of Ka-Nying Shedrub Ling Monastery in Kathmandu, he has extensive knowledge of the esoteric Vajrayana Buddhist methods. Nonetheless,

Rinpoche often bases his instructions on the words of the Buddha as expressed in the sutras. He integrates the vast view of the Great Perfection, the uncontrived meditation of Mahamudra, and the Mahayana teachings on wisdom and compassion.

Phakchok Rinpoche directs a range of humanitarian projects in South Asia, heads translation initiatives through Lhasey Lotsawa Translations and Publications, and offers a wealth of Buddhist resources and programs through Samye Institute. More information on Rinpoche and his activities can be found at phakchokrinpoche.org.